How Long Have I Got?

How Long
Have I Got?

The Story of a 'Terminal' Cancer Patient

Fi Munro Ph.D.

Cover Design: Victoria Wylie Hale

ISBN: 9781790572915

www.fkmunro.com

First Edition: August 2017 (Previously entitled *Love, Light and Mermaid Tails*)
Second Edition: January 2019

10 9 8 7 6 5 4 3 2 1

PRAISE FOR *FI MUNRO, PH.D.*

'Please read *'How Long Have I Got?'* Fi has courageously chosen to share her experiences of becoming a warrior - of HAVING to become a warrior. Of having to almost fight for a correct diagnosis of ovarian cancer... and then to fight on with her own extraordinary armoury: joy, light and love. Her generosity in sharing her every step knows no bounds. If you or someone you know has just received a frightening diagnosis - please have this book as your lifeline. I wish my family had had the gift of Fi's beautifully written account eight years ago when the symptoms of my mother's ovarian cancer were dismissed. No more of 'brushing off'. No more dismissal. No more leaving the doctor's surgery without getting that referral for a scan, exam or test. Take courage and heart from Fi Munro. Oh yes, she'll make you laugh too.' - **Sarah Greene**, television personality

'Fi is a true cancer warrior and thriver. She has been to the brink, undergone potentially catastrophic surgery and emerged more herself than before. She finds light in darkness.' - **Sophie Sabbage**, bestselling author of The Cancer Whisperer and Lifeshocks - And How to Love Them

'Cancer is a scary word for most people. Putting 'ovarian' before it makes many clinicians sigh deeply because of the tough prognosis. Diagnosis often comes late. Raising awareness is vital and that's why wonderful women like Fi telling their stories is at the heart of what we do as a charity. Fi doesn't ask 'why me?' (statistically it really shouldn't be her), her call to arms is: 'this could be any of us so what can we all do?' Above everything, Fi shows us how to live well with cancer, not to be defined as potentially dying from it.' - **Athena Lamnisos**, CEO of The Eve Appeal

'Fi a rare flashlight in the tunnel of illness. She shows it's possible to live an extraordinary life with cancer. She empowers, inspires and fills me with hope. We're all alive, but how many of us are truly living? Fi's story could save lives and transform beliefs.' - **Sophie Trew**, founder of Trew Fields Festival, a ground breaking cancer awareness and holistic health event

'This book is a powerhouse of useful information from the front lines of a cancer journey. Truth, honesty and practicality shine through; it's a must read for anyone experiencing or supporting a similar journey.' - **Rhonda McCrimmon**, The Travelling Shaman

'Using her values as a compass Fi shares a message of hope, not fear, about how you can heal your life even if you can't be cured. A powerful message for us all.' - **Lesley Howells**, Consultant Clinical Psychologist and Centre Head, Maggie's

'Fi is one of the most incredible people I've ever met. She has not only brought us all a game changer of a book, it's also filled with love, positivity, humor, practical insight and huge awareness of what cancer does to the body and mind. It's a book that changed my life and I now recommend it to everyone.' - **Tina McGuff**, best-selling author of Seconds to Snap

'Fi made a choice to take a leap and live in her heart. Her heart centred wisdom, coupled with her fastidious approach to research makes the very best combination. Fi's book is a generous, hearted and beautiful gift for human kind.' - **Dr Kate James**, Integrated Medicine Doctor

'Fi brings her distinctive voice and perpetual positivity to this wonderful book. Fi and Target Ovarian Cancer share a goal of raising awareness of ovarian cancer, yes – but more than that, of showing the world that you can live a full life after a diagnosis. She is an incredible, inspirational member of a wonderful community and I am full of admiration for all that she does.' - **Annwen Jones**, Chief Executive of Target Ovarian Cancer

For my fellow teal warriors. You are not alone.

'In order to heal you must send out healing.
In order to forgive you must seek forgiveness.
In order to be loved you must send out love.
In order to shine you must send out light.
When you heal the whole world heals, because we are all connected.
When one person shows that healing is possible, they show others to
know this too. This is your purpose. You are already healed.
Now you must show others the way. Your purpose is to show others
that they can heal. Do not feel guilt for your healing for it is what
your soul asked for. Your soul asked for the struggle in this life so
that it could grow and help others.
From the moment of conception, when your soul had to survive the
binding of your mother's womb, it was all leading to this point. Feel
gratitude for the pain, for you were learning and it led you to this
point so that you could help others to see the light.
You are here to guide them. You are here to give hope.
Know that you are healed.
Know that all is well and you have nothing to fear.
Forgive yourself and allow the tentacles of past emotions to release
you and, in doing so, also release your tentacles that hold on to
others from your past.
Let them go, forgive yourself and know that all is well.
Now is your time to show the possibilities. Embrace them.
Open your heart.
You are already healed.
Replace fear, anger and anxiety with gratitude, love and light.
All is well.
You are here to live a long life following this purpose and this path.
Keep sharing hope and guide the way and you will remain healed.
Feel joy.
Feel laughter.
Feel love.'
~ A message from my soul to yours, Fi Munro ~

CONTENTS

PART 4: Awakening Your Healing Power

PART 5: Cancer is My Guru

FOREWORD

It is by observing people who do exceptional things and follow exceptional paths that we can learn the most. Fi Munro is one of these people.

Fi made a choice to take a leap and live in her heart. Within its sacred space she has found answers she would otherwise have not, a different path to the more ordinary. Her story is a story of a courageous Creatress, a fearless dancing 'Dakini' co-creating with the Universe.

I have been a medical doctor for almost two decades and have had the privilege to watch how differently life may play out when we find and make choices from the sacred space within our hearts. When we honour its wisdom and messages in each and every moment we can experience insurmountable strength and support and also find our true path.

Fifteen years ago I went on my own journey with the two most important women in my life, first helping support my Mum who was diagnosed with locally advanced breast cancer, and two years later my daughter who was diagnosed with an infant leaukaemia.

I was able to support both of them holistically alongside their conventional oncology treatment as I let my heart and instinct guide me as I trawled through the available evidence in the Integrative Oncology field.

Both Grace and my Mum thankfully made a full recovery. I underwent a metamorphosis during their journeys. I realised the only way to live and work was from my heart. I left Accident and Emergency Medicine and began to practice Integrative Medicine. I too learned to follow my heart.

Fi's book is a generous, hearted and beautiful gift for human kind. She very naturally found her heart space and is clearly an incredible student! Her tips and tools help those of us for whom perhaps finding this space is a little more tricky. However by sharing in the heart centred experiences and journeys of others it always gets easier to live in our own.

Fi's heart centred wisdom, coupled with her fastidious approach to research makes the very best combination. Thank you, Fi, for being you and for following your heart.

Dr Kate James

AUTHOR'S NOTE

Some of you may have already read the first edition of this book - previously entitled *Love, Light and Mermaid Tails*. I published that edition just 18 months before this one and yet I have learnt so much in that short time. Life, as it does, continued to serve me many lessons that I now hope to share with you all.

In the first edition I detailed my survival of a physically abusive relationship, a ruptured ectopic pregnancy, stage four cancer, major surgery and more. Above all, I shared how these moments had shaped me.

Since then, however, my cancer has returned. This time it was more aggressive and at many stages in the past year my situation became critical. In truth, there were many moments I didn't think I would survive. I was being called to go deeper on my journey as I awakened the healing power within and truly became the warrior I was destined to be.

Many of you already know that I've never discussed my prognosis with my oncologist. I don't want to be labelled as a statistic and I don't think it's fair on them, or me, to have predictions made that no one can realistically make. The title of this book, therefore, is not a reflection of asking my oncologist that question, but rather of me asking myself it every morning. It is what makes me appreciate the preciousness of life and what encourages me to keep pursuing my dreams.

When I was first diagnosed with cancer in early 2016 it was already stage four. There is no stage five. At the time of diagnosis my cancer was classed as terminal. I was just 30 years old.

Suddenly, everything I had identified as 'me' came to a stand still. In one moment, after months of pain, tests and assurances that it was 'nothing to worry about', my instincts were proved right and my worst fears were realised.

Medically speaking, I was dying.

In the months that followed I wanted to hear inspirational stories of hope, love and possibility from fellow late stage cancer warriors. As I searched, however, I found that most of the inspirational stories of positivity following a cancer diagnosis are from those with an early, curable diagnosis. Of course they are positive; they knew they were going to live! 'Where were all the warriors in a similar situation to me?' I wondered. 'Why is no one writing positive experiences about life with incurable cancer?'

It was in that moment that I realised I wanted to share my story more publicly. I realised that I had the opportunity to spread a message of hope, not one of fear. I had the chance to challenge the media driven perception that cancer should happen behind closed doors and that cancer patients lose their lives the moment they are diagnosed. I wanted to show people that I was still living. I wanted to show them that there is still life after a cancer diagnosis and, as it happens, it can be a great life.

The media would have you believe that us late stage cancer warriors are all too sick to be living positive lives and that cancer, having consumed our body, is now consuming our lives and that we are simply waiting to die.

I want to break down this perception. I want people to see that not only can you live with cancer but that your life can be amazing!

We all face adversity. Each and every day brings new challenges and sometimes despair. But life is a gift and an adventure waiting to be embraced and enjoyed. It *is* possible to live a grateful life even when going through adversity. At any given moment you can decide 'this is not how my story ends' and begin to rewrite your story.

Cancer taught me how to live a deep and fulfilling life. Rather than making me fear my death, it has taught me how to love my life and how to live each day full of joy and laughter. It has also led me to discover the disease that filled every corner of my life: the emotional traumas I hadn't dealt with; the chemicals that fill our beautiful world; the modern obsession with status and appearance; the lack of joy; and so much more!

I know now that I am here to write *this* book, to share with you the messages I have gathered and the lessons I have learned that have enabled me to live such a wonderful and fulfilling life in the face of death.

I am here to serve you, to guide you, to help you on your journey back to wholeness and to help you to see through the illusions created by our modern society, to enable you to break free and to find the best version of yourself that your inner spirit longs for you to become.

I wrote this book to share my story with you and to offer encouragement and reassurance. It is my message of hope for anyone facing adversity. It tells my story and how I have used love, hope and positivity to get me through my journey.

I hope my words will demonstrate that no matter how bad it gets, how dark the situation, or how impossible the odds, there is always hope. If nothing else, I wish that as you read my words that you never lose sight of that beautiful fact.

We are all in this together and I am holding and honouring your energy as I see you whole and healed today, and always, in this life and the next.

May my words bring you love, peace and, above all, joy.

Love, light and healing always, Fi xx

INTRODUCTION: THE COST OF SUCCESS

By society's standards, my life before cancer was great. Ambitious from a young age, I had completed my PhD a few months shy of my 26th birthday and had since dedicated my working life to a career as a researcher. My passion for improving the healthcare system and promoting holistic health and wellbeing motivated me to juggle a 140 mile daily commute, a full time job, volunteering and part-time study to train as a psychotherapist.

My 'spare time' (I use that term loosely) was spent exercising. I was passionate about running and lifting weights and attended regular fitness classes and personal training sessions. Admittedly I got a huge buzz from the challenge, the pain and the competitive nature of training.

On the surface I had 'optimal health'. I exercised daily, I ate healthily, I never smoked and I very rarely drank and never in excess. Yet, somehow, I still found myself facing a death sentence at just the age of 30. What had gone wrong?

A cancer diagnosis doesn't start the day you're told you have cancer. It's not a simple case of one day you don't have cancer and the next you do. No, the journey starts long before that. In fact, recent research studies indicate that most cancers are growing in the body undetected for up to eight years before a diagnosis.

Of course, cancer gently whispers to us for months (if not years) before we seek answers that will lead to a diagnosis. Not that we ever listen to those first whispers. No, we are far too busy living for 'nonsense' like that.

My first whisper came in October 2013, more than two years before my diagnosis.

I was busy with preparations for our wedding, which was due to take place just two months later. I was marrying my best friend and I couldn't wait. Everything was in place and, as far as any bride can be, I was relaxed and calm. (Well, that's my story and I'm sticking to it - my husband, of course, may have a different opinion about my stress levels.)

I'd spent the previous six months training for the 2014 London Marathon, having secured a rare place through a charity. I'd dedicated each day to running at least three miles, lifting weights and seeing my personal trainer. Yes, this was while also doing a daily three-hour commute, a full time stressful job and planning an imminent wedding. Success comes at a price don't you know? At least that's what I had thought at the time. It's now, however, a price I'm no longer willing to pay.

To say I was putting myself under unnecessary pressure would be the ultimate understatement, but I didn't see that. To look at me I was the vision of impeccable health and even had some subtle abdominal muscles to show for it. Weight was falling off of me and at each dress fitting my wedding dress needed altered, much to the annoyance of the seamstress. I thought I was happy and society encouraged this. A day didn't pass where I wasn't rewarded with comments of praise and admiration for juggling life and spinning every plate imaginable. Well-meaning phrases like 'I don't know how you do it. It's incredible' became the norm for me and I felt encouraged to do more, to push more, to keep trying harder at all costs.

Then, one Sunday while on an early morning run a speeding car on the wrong side of the road knocked me down. I hit my head as I fell and a hospital visit confirmed I had a mild concussion. I was told that I needed to rest. However, at this stage there was no stopping me. Against medical advice, I continued to train after only a couple of days on the sofa. Something was different though. On my third run following the accident my left leg gave way and I had to call my husband to collect me. Then, in the days that followed my left hip began to cause me constant pain, even while resting. Within a couple of weeks I was unable to exercise at all and using crutches every day. I was devastated. Exercise was my life. I felt so lost.

Over the following months I had regular ultrasounds, x-rays, an MRI and steroid injections into my hip joint. However, no one could pinpoint the exact cause of my pain. They did, however, note at the time that my left ovary was enlarged and my bloods were showing elevated hormone levels and a high white blood count.

'It's just your age,' I was told. 'Nothing to worry about and definitely not the cause of your hip pain.' On reflection now, I'm not so sure. Research indicates that hip pain is one of the first symptoms of ovarian cancer, not to mention that my enlarged ovary should have been a warning sign.

Over the course of the following year I had a steroid injection into my hip every time the pain reached a point where I couldn't go about my day-to-day activities. Exercise was a thing of the past and, regrettably, I withdrew my place in London Marathon.

Fast forward a year and I was a very different person. By early 2015 I was tired all of the time, gaining weight and super stressed and irritable. I binged on sugar daily, sometimes eating my entire daily-recommended calorie allowance in sweets and chocolate, in addition to three large meals. As a result, I no longer recognised the person I saw in the mirror. Long gone was my athletic frame and, although I was still only a petite size 12, I was disgusted about my health. The praise I had learnt to crave no longer came and a dark cloud of self-loathing consumed me.

Around the same time my husband and I began making plans to start a family. We had now been married for over a year and the time felt right. It was a new chapter and I felt excited about the prospect of something positive to focus on.

As soon as I stopped taking the contraceptive pill, however, I was in constant pain. My hip started hurting again, my abdomen was constantly bloated and I was frequently experiencing spasm-like pain.

'It's just your body readjusting,' I was told by my GP. 'It'll pass.'

Then, in July 2015, my dreams came true. I finally discovered I was pregnant.

I'd just about given up all hope of it ever happening. The stress had become all-consuming, as frustration and anxiety filled my every thought. Yet, there we were staring at a positive pregnancy test. We were finally about to become parents. I didn't know whether to laugh or cry. I was so excited!

A follow up pregnancy test, however, was negative.

'It's just a miscarriage. It's perfectly normal,' came the GP's dismissive response to my concerns. 'Such a shame, really' she added, 'I'd been looking forward to some good news today. Go home and rest. You'll probably have some bleeding, but that's perfectly normal.'

I was devastated. 'Perfectly normal?' I thought. 'How could something so awful be normal?'

I'm not sure if it was instinct or denial but something wasn't sitting right with me. I wasn't convinced I was having a miscarriage and so I took a third test. This one was positive.

I needed answers and, feeling unsupported by my then GP (I now have a different one), I called the Early Pregnancy Unit at my local hospital.

'Come in and we'll have a look at you,' came the warm response of the midwife who answered the phone.

I went in with my husband and they took some blood tests and performed an internal ultrasound. This confirmed that I was pregnant but that there was a risk of a miscarriage. We were due to go away on holiday to northern Scotland the following week but I was terrified about leaving.

'Just go and try your best to relax. There is nothing you can do to change what will happen. Your body will decide.' The midwife's honesty was comforting and, although I was still scared, I knew I was now in safe hands.

Our holiday, as predicted, was awful. I was in constant pain and needing to urinate every few minutes. I started to lose blood and I knew we were probably going to lose our baby. My husband offered constant reassurance. I didn't want reassured though. I wanted to be excited like other couples get to be. I wanted to tell everyone we had amazing news. The last thing I wanted to do was to just sit and wait for nature to decide. More than anything I wanted to be home so that I could go and speak to the midwives again. I needed their reassurance. I needed to know that everything was going to be okay.

On our last day my husband and I visited the most beautiful beach. I grew up in the Channel Islands and so as soon as I step onto a beach I'm like a six year old, laughing and running about barefoot in the sand. I felt free and for the first time that week I wasn't obsessing about hospitals or pregnancy. I was a wife on holiday with her husband, loving her life. It was a beautiful moment.

On our way home, however, I became doubled over in pain in the car. Stopping at a service station, I went to the toilet to discover heavy blood loss. There was blood everywhere. I burst into tears.

We drove to the nearest hospital and went straight to A&E, where I was seen immediately and told that I needed to be taken in an ambulance to a larger hospital. 'It's probably just a miscarriage, but we are concerned that it might be ectopic,' the student nurse explained 'we need to get you seen by a consultant.'

'Ectopic.' The word hung in the air as she left. Due to increasing abdominal pains, I'd been saying for the past week that I thought it was an ectopic pregnancy but had been reassured that this would have been picked up on the ultrasound.

'I'm not convinced that it's even a miscarriage, let alone an ectopic,' explained the consultant after she'd examined me at the larger hospital. 'It could just be an implantation bleed.' I looked at her in disbelief. She had to be kidding. I must have lost about half a pint of blood.

'Go home and relax and come back tomorrow.'

'Relax?' I thought to myself. How could I possibly

relax?

The following day brought more questions. My pregnancy hormone had risen and not fallen, as would have been expected if I'd had a miscarriage. However, a scan was showing nothing in my womb.

'We'll do a blood test every forty-eight hours to monitor your pregnancy hormone levels,' was the only solution they could muster. 'Promise us that you'll come in immediately if you experience any sudden abdominal pain.'

So, for over a week I went into hospital every two days for blood tests. My hormone levels continued to rise but not at a level that would be considered 'normal' for a viable pregnancy.

Then, a third scan answered the question that had now been left unanswered for three weeks. 'The embryo is sitting in your left fallopian tube. I'm sorry, but you have an ectopic pregnancy.' It was a mixture of distress and relief. At least I finally had an answer.

'You'll need to make a decision about how you want to terminate the pregnancy. You can either take a drug that contains chemotherapy or you can have surgery.'

'I want surgery,' I stated without thought.

'The risks are quite serious. Are you sure?'

'Yes.' Instinct was kicking in and I knew it was what needed to be done. I'd known it was an ectopic pregnancy before they had and so I knew I had to listen to my body again.

'Why don't you sleep on it and come back first thing tomorrow. We'll prep you for surgery but you can change your mind at any stage.'

The following morning I was terrified. I'd been told that I could haemorrhage during surgery or that they could even rupture my bladder or bowel. There were so many risks associated with surgery whereas the drug they had offered, which I'd been told would 'destroy the foetus', had minimal risks.

I made a desperate deal with the universe. 'If I hear a Michael Jackson song before they ask me again then I'll have surgery. If not then I won't.' It seems stupid when recalling this desperation now, but I've been making silent pleas like this my whole life.

When we arrived we were told to sit in the waiting room where, on previous visits, the TV had been blasting daytime TV programmes. However, we were in earlier than normal and the radio was on. Michael Jackson's 'Beat It' was playing as we entered the room and my mind was made. I was having surgery. However, I still had reservations.

'What if I don't wake up?' I asked my husband as he held me close in the moments before I was taken to theatre.

'You will. Don't be daft. I'll see you soon,' came his response. I was aware, however, that he held me just a little tighter than usual before leaving the room.

Following surgery I drifted in and out of consciousness in the recovery room. The registrar was standing beside me and kept touching my arm.

Once fully awake and in a hospital side-room the surgeon came to see me. 'Well you're certainly the talk of the hospital today,' she laughed.

'Why?' I asked still groggy from the anaesthetic and not sure what she was on about.

'Has no one told you?' she asked confused. 'Your heart stopped when they gave you the anaesthetic. They managed to give you an adrenalin shot and get you breathing again. Just as well really. You were so low risk for this happening that the adrenalin was locked in a cupboard. You didn't half give us all a fright.'

'Why did it happen?' I managed to mutter.

Was I hearing her right? My heart had stopped? That couldn't be true.

'You had a ruptured ectopic pregnancy. Just as well you chose surgery. You had internal bleeding from your left fallopian tube. Goodness knows what would have happened if we'd just sent you home with medication.' She laughed again. This time I realised it was nervous laughter. 'The anaesthetist will be in later to chat to you about it all. In the meantime just rest.'

'I medically died.' I thought to myself as she left the

room. But? What? I couldn't even begin to comprehend what was happening.

Hours later the anaesthesia team were sitting in front of my husband and I explaining everything in detail. There were lots of apologies and reassurances but I wasn't really listening. Dying is one thing but getting to live afterwards - now that deserved some reflection.

Regrettably I didn't fully appreciate this gift and, as a result, I missed the opportunity to live with any new insight. The lessons I would later learn following my cancer diagnosis (and now hope to share with you, my reader) hadn't taken effect and instead I wallowed in grief over our loss. Within a couple of weeks I'd immersed myself back into my work and was focusing all of my spare time on intensive exercise again.

Reflecting on this now I realise that I was looking for a distraction, a way out from the pain I was feeling. I was seeking an escape rather than acceptance. However, instead of doing what my body needed and letting myself grieve and giving myself the time and space to emotionally and physically heal, I began to punish myself with intensified self-loathing. I was in a very dark place.

To make matters worse, during this time I was experiencing constant abdominal pain, swelling and frequent urination and so I went to see my GP on a number of occasions over an eight-week period. She would always reassure me that my symptoms were due to irritation caused by the internal bleeding while delicately asking if I thought I needed emotional support to get me through this time.

'No, I'm fine,' always came my reply. It was a vain attempt at convincing myself that I was doing well; that I was coping.

Other symptoms started to plague me too. My right rib cage was causing me constant pain, my sternum ached and, on one particular day, I collapsed in our hallway for no apparent reason.

'You're just overdoing it with the exercises you're doing. Perhaps you should take some time to rest.'

I wasn't convinced.

My concerns increasingly grew when a lump started to form around one of the surgical scars in my abdomen.

'It's just scar tissue from your operation. Try not to worry,' the GP assured me gently.

'It's growing though, scar tissue doesn't grow.' I insisted.

'I don't think it is growing. You've been through a lot this year. Are you sure you don't want to speak to someone about how you are feeling?'

'No.' I left her office feeling alone. Why was no one taking my concerns seriously?

However, when I didn't stop going to see my GP she finally agreed to help alleviate my concerns and referred me for an ultrasound of my abdomen.

Weeks later, in November 2015 the radiologist noted that I had large cysts on both of my ovaries, each measuring over five centimeters across. She also noted that one looked 'suspicious' and that perhaps a post-surgery infection was responsible for my symptoms.

In response to this I mentioned my family history of ovarian and breast cancer and asked if she thought I should be concerned. Just like with my ectopic pregnancy, instinct was again taking over. I knew something was wrong just like I had known I needed surgery. However, she said it was unlikely at my age but that she would refer me to see a consultant gynaecologist and arrange for my GP to take a CA125 blood test. This, she explained, was an ovarian cancer marker test. A high number may indicate the need for further tests. She didn't need to explain this to me. I already knew. I'd been researching ovarian cancer for the past two months due to my increasing concern that this was the cause of my distress and symptoms.

I first saw my consultant gynaecologist in early December 2015. He confirmed that my CA125 blood test results were elevated but that he was not concerned because this can also indicate an infection. Instead he began asking about sexual partners and said he was going to test me for STIs.

'I've been with my husband for seven years. There is no risk of an STI.'

'You'd be surprised,' he laughed, testing me anyway.

'Are you sure it's not ovarian cancer? I have all the

symptoms and we have a family history of the disease.'

'Definitely not. You have no risk of ovarian cancer. You're too young. Did you receive psychiatric support after your 'episode' in the summer? I'm sure you are just overly concerned as a result.'

I wasn't sure if he was referring to the ruptured ectopic, losing a child, my heart stopping during surgery or all of the above. Either way, I was offended and made a decision that I neither liked nor trusted this man who at that moment was now conducting a rather painful internal examination with his hands without explanation.

'Come back in a few weeks. I'm sure your symptoms will have passed by then.'
I left feeling dissatisfied and annoyed. I went to see my GP as soon as possible, voicing my concerns.

'Fiona, he's written down everything you said to him in a letter he sent me. He mentions your concern about ovarian cancer and highlights that there is no risk,' she reassured me. 'I have to say I'm relieved. I thought to myself this poor girl has just had an ectopic pregnancy, surely she can't be unlucky enough to have ovarian cancer too' she smiled, reassuring me. 'Why don't you go to your next appointment with him and if you are still not happy then we will look at other options. Okay?'

'Okay.' I liked her. At least she listened.

Over the next few weeks my husband and I, with medical permission, celebrated our wedding anniversary in Vienna, however, my abdominal swelling had now reached a point where I was unable to eat and I was growing increasingly anxious about my health. Worse case scenarios consumed my thoughts and fear filled my mind.

When I returned to see the gynaecologist he tried to reassure me, letting me know that all of my tests had come back clear from infection and asked if my symptoms had passed. I explained that they had progressed and so he conducted an ultrasound. This was the first time he'd scanned me, having dismissed my requests at our previous appointment despite the fact that he hadn't seen the scan the radiologist had done previously.

Following this he explained that he would repeat the CA125 test to eliminate ovarian cancer as a risk factor, reassuring me that he still thought I had a post-surgery infection.

However, at a follow-up appointment a week later he let me know that my CA125 test results had risen.

'I've met with the surgeon who operated on you in the summer. She's assured me that if you had ovarian cancer that it would have been picked up at the time of your operation. However, I think it's best that we book you in for a laparoscopy in late January. Do come back if your symptoms get worse in the meantime.' He handed me a note of his email address before showing me out. I couldn't help but notice that his manner was different this time.

'I thought you said I was too young for ovarian cancer?' I asked.

'There are rare cases,' he explained. 'I'm not worried but it might be best to eliminate it as a possible factor'. I couldn't help but reflect that this was exactly what I'd been asking him to do for several weeks now.

Two weeks later, however, while at work and over 70 miles from the hospital in which my gynaecologist worked, my abdominal swelling and pain got to the stage that I was unable to do anything. Lying on a couch at the far end of the office, I used my phone to email him, stating that I thought something was seriously wrong.

Moments later my phone rang. 'Come in straight away,' came his voice on the other end of the line.

I drove myself the 70 miles from my place of work to my local hospital and by the time I arrived it was after hours but he had waited. He conducted another ultrasound. This time it clearly showed a build-up of fluid around my abdominal organs. His reassurances stopped and I was worried.

'We need to do an abdominal drain straight away so you'll need to stay in overnight. Can someone bring in some things for you?'

'My husband.' Was all I managed to answer despite the hundreds of questions running through my head.

That night five litres of fluid, weighing 5kg, were drained from my abdominal cavity. Having spent the previous few months concerned that I was gaining weight despite my intense exercise routine, this revealed that, in reality, I had been losing weight at a rapid rate. By the time the drain was complete my ribs and hips were clearly visible. I was skin and bone.

There was no more talk about STIs or imagined symptoms. Something had changed. However, I was still assured that this was a sign of a serious post-surgery infection and not cancer.

The next day I was discharged with several boxes of oral antibiotics to take over the weekend and asked to come back into hospital the following week for an MRI while they waited for the lab to do tests on the fluid they had drained.

The MRI took place four days later, following which I was told that the fluid had tested clear from infection and that the lab were conducting further tests. I was not surprised it had shown no signs of infection. My blood results the previous week had been clear from infection too and I was now increasingly concerned that I had ovarian cancer. I again voiced my fears to my gynaecologist.

'We need to run some further tests on the fluid. Your MRI is showing a mass in your abdomen but, at this stage, we are not sure of the cause. I'll phone you as soon as I have more information about your results. In the meantime, you can go home and rest.'

It's odd, but I knew. I knew I had cancer. I'd always known. There was a difference now though. Now his eyes told me that he knew too.

Less than 30 minutes later, while sitting in my car in

a supermarket car park, I received the call that would change my life.

'Can you come into the hospital this afternoon?'

'Yes. Why?'

'We have your lab results. I think it would be best if you could bring someone with you.' He said, without answering my question.

He didn't need to say any more. I'd been speaking to this consultant nearly every day for two weeks and he always told me everything over the phone. Although he didn't confirm anything during the call I knew in that moment that the further tests had confirmed my worst fears. I knew they'd found ovarian cancer cells. I knew my life was changing forever.

I cried all the way home.

PART ONE

THE WAKE UP CALL

CHAPTER 1: 'YOU HAVE CANCER.'

January 18ᵗʰ 2016

I'll never forget that moment. The moment my life changed forever. The moment 'cancer' entered my world. I was sitting next to my husband in a cold hospital room. The consultant gynaecologist was sitting in front of my husband and me with his head in his hands. Just weeks earlier he'd told me that there was nothing serious to worry about and yet there we were, moments into the New Year and I was being told that not only did I have cancer, but that it had spread.

My prognosis wasn't great.

'I'll give you a minute,' the consultant continued as he left the room, not knowing what else to say to the young couple sat before him.

My husband was sat motionless, his face grey with shock and disbelief. I wasn't shocked, however. I'd known deep down that something seriously wasn't right with my body. It's why I'd gone back and forth seeking medical answers for the previous few months since my ectopic pregnancy. As a result I admit to experiencing a level of relief from his words. At least I hadn't been imagining my many symptoms, as some of the health professionals I'd seen had insinuated.

As I turned to face my husband I saw a broken man. Looking up to meet my gaze, his eyes begged me to say something to take away the pain. I knew I had a choice. I knew that moment would determine our future. I could either succumb to what we'd just been told, accepting my fate as a 'terminally ill patient', or I could use every ounce of positivity I had left to keep going.

I, of course, chose the latter. I wasn't prepared to become a victim. I was only 30 years old after all. I wasn't prepared to die.

'At least we can get a dog,' I laugh. My dark sense of humor perhaps more than a little out of place at that moment.

'What?' my husband stuttered back at me.

'A dog,' I said more confidently and with a little laugh. 'I've wanted one for ages and we couldn't get one before because of work, but he just said I can't work now.'

My husband laughed and took me in his arms. In doing so the tension and sadness in the room shifted.

'Okay, you can get a dog.'[1]

* * *

I don't remember how long we sat there holding each other, but I know that I wanted to leave as soon as possible. I had to tell people. I wanted it out. I wanted to scream it from the rooftops. It was like, in that moment, speaking the words would release me from the pain I was feeling inside.

There is a famous thought experiment (or paradox) devised by Austrian physicist Erwin Schrödinger that presents a cat in a closed box with poison. In the scenario, the cat is dead if it has consumed the poison and alive if it has not. However, until the box is opened either option is still likely. That is, the cat may be simultaneously both alive and dead. This is a state known as a quantum superposition.

'That's all very well and interesting but what does it have to do with the story we are in the middle of?' I'm sure you're thinking. Well, as it happens, everything. You see, in those moments following my cancer diagnosis my hubby and me had, unknowingly, entered our own quantum superposition. While we both knew I had cancer, none of our loved ones knew. In those moments before they heard the news, two realities coexisted. One in which I had cancer and one in which I did not.

For me, I only wanted there to be one reality and, as it

---

[1] *In February 2016 we welcomed Robbie, a thirteen-year-old cocker spaniel, into our home from a local dog rescue center. His previous owner had passed away and he was looking for a new home. After a wonderful, but short, ten months with us, Robbie passed away in my arms in December 2016.*

couldn't be the reality where I was healthy, I wanted all of our loved ones in the same reality as us. I soon discovered, however, that the hardest part of having cancer isn't hearing your diagnosis; it's having to tell the people you love; it's having to hear them muffle their tears as they try to stay strong for you; it's having to break so many hearts. That's where the real pain comes from.

My family and friends rallied around as always and I felt an overwhelming sense of support and love. I spent the evening phoning and texting close friends and sitting with my sisters in my parents' home. My parents were on holiday in Spain and so I had to tell them over the phone. That was the hardest call I've ever had to make. How do you tell two loving parents that their youngest has cancer? Worse still, how do you do this over the phone and not face to face where they can hold you in their arms?

I left my husband alone in our home while I sat with my sisters. This wasn't out of lack of love but in fact, the complete opposite. My husband is my soul mate, my best friend and my other half. I couldn't bear to see my pain reflected in his eyes. I couldn't stand the thought of the suffering I was putting him through. Guilt washed over me in his presence. I didn't want to face the grief, the hurt or the guilt that was consuming me. To this day I regret this decision. I wish I'd stayed at home. I wish I'd sat in his arms that night, silently absorbing his love. I wish I'd stayed inside our own quantum superposition for just a little while longer.

When I returned home I finally let myself settle in his arms on our sofa. I felt safe. In his arms it was like the diagnosis didn't exist, like it didn't matter. I knew that together we would get through it and that, whatever the outcome, we would love and support each other every day. For the first time, I let the reality of my diagnosis wash over me and my tears fell freely. This acceptance was an important step. I was acknowledging the reality. I was not letting the grief consume me but rather letting it wash over me and, in doing so, I was letting it pass.

In the days and weeks following a diagnosis it can be so hard to adjust to the 'new normal' and emotions can be all over the place. However, there is no right or wrong way to feel. People shouldn't expect to feel sad all the time. Neither, of course, should they expect to feel happy all of the time. Instead, these feelings ebb and flow with each changing moment like the waves on a shore.

The following day I was to be admitted to hospital for further tests. I woke feeling strong and determined. A sense of relief hung in the air. It was the start of my journey and this gave me strength.

I'd told my husband that, not knowing how long I would be in hospital for, I wanted to go for a walk on my favourite beach. It's funny how, less than 24 hours after my diagnosis, cancer was already opening my eyes to what mattered most. In its own way, it was already creating a value for little things that I had previously lost. Sadly, time seemed to pass faster than normal and we only had time for a walk around our local fields. However, it was still magical to feel the fresh air fill my lungs as I absorbed the countryside views. Walking hand in hand with my husband I was not a 'cancer patient', I was a young woman, a wife, a friend, a daughter, a sister and an aunt. I was me. I recognised the importance of connecting with my sense of self in this moment, realising it would serve me well over the coming months as I strived to maintain my identity in a large system seemingly designed to do the exact opposite.

During that walk we took a photo. Looking at it now I see we are both smiling at the camera. An observer wouldn't know the pain that had just entered our world. Instead they would see a couple deeply in love with each other. In that moment we captured the strength that my diagnosis had given us, our determination to be together and the undying love we held for each other.

I posted that picture on social media when I announced I had been diagnosed with cancer. The response from online friends was incredible. In a world where we often see hate and fear plastered on our screens and newspapers, I was suddenly held in a bubble of love. Messages poured in from a range of people who, at various stages, had touched both of our lives over the years. Each message was filled with hope, comfort and support.

When we arrived at the hospital I was admitted to the gynaecology ward. I was told that I wasn't to be admitted to the oncology ward at this stage because, I quote, they 'didn't think I was ready'. While this may have been the case, these words stuck with me and I became terrified about what the oncology ward might hold. Images of extremely sick people, without hair, their bodies just skin and bone, attached to tubes leading to various machines filled my mind. In reality the oncology ward is a beautiful place filled with love and support and I can now attest with utter confidence that it is a place in which I feel deeply cared for and supported. Also, needless to say, in the coming months the very image that filled my mind with fear became the same image I saw in the mirror and, although hard of course, it was not as frightening as I had once imagined. There is something about the progression of a cancer journey that almost prepares you for each phase (more on this later).

At this time in my journey the medical priority was to 'stage' my cancer. This basically meant that they wanted to see how far it had spread throughout my body.

It was a frightening prospect. The stages of cancer weren't something that had ever really crossed my mind in the past. I'd always thought you either had cancer or you didn't. However, some overnight reading had shown that most cancers have four stages and that each of these stages are often broken down into A, B and C. So, for example, Stage 1A is the earliest stage of cancer and occurs when the cancer has not spread beyond the primary site. For instance, in ovarian cancer this would mean that the cancer was just in one ovary. In cases like this the cancer is often treated with surgery to remove the affected ovary and further treatment like chemotherapy isn't often required. Stage 4C however is the opposite. This diagnosis indicates that the cancer has spread throughout the organs in the abdominal cavity and into the organs in the chest cavity. Treatment, if possible, is intense and used only to make the patient more comfortable. At this stage the cancer is no longer curable. My cancer was Stage 4B at the point of diagnosis. I was medically 'f**ked'.

Sadly, with ovarian cancer, women are often only

diagnosed at a later stage due to the fact that there are no routine screening tests for ovarian cancer. Indeed, despite the common misconception that smear tests look for ovarian cancer this is in fact not the case and is, in reality, anatomically impossible.

The consultant who diagnosed me had already told me that 'due to the progressive symptoms' I was demonstrating, it was likely that my cancer had spread to an advanced stage. At the time of hearing those words I didn't fully appreciate what this meant but the look on his face had said it all. I knew it wasn't good news.

I had a CT scan booked for that afternoon. It felt like the longest wait I'd ever had. I just wanted it to be over with so that I could hear the results. The nursing staff explained that often the results take weeks but that 'given the circumstances' they hoped to get the initial results to me as soon as possible.

Their words had been intended to comfort me but instead they reconfirmed that my situation wasn't ideal to say the least.

While I waited my sisters and husband sat with me. I was glad they were all there, not just for me but also for each other. It gave me comfort to know that none of them were going through this alone. At the time my parents were still en-route back from Spain having driven through the night.

There was almost a sense of relief in going for my CT scan. It may sound crazy but I knew it was taking me one step closer to my recovery and although I knew it was likely to uncover news I didn't want to hear, it was all part of a necessary process. I knew I couldn't truly accept the news until I had all the facts.

I have since learnt that many people don't want to hear the stage of their cancer. I respect this completely. For me, however, I needed the clarity. Knowing gave me all of the facts (good and bad) about my body and allowed me to remain in control of what was happening to me. This enabled me to be involved in the decisions around my treatment and helped me to maintain my identity as much as possible. This control was a vital part of my recovery and, also, my unwavering positivity. Whatever the medical team had to tell me, the thoughts in my imagination were always worse! Knowledge truly became my power.

Despite all this, however, nothing prepared me for the emotions I felt during my CT scan. Having stayed strong during the months of testing and the previous 24 hours since diagnosis, when I was taken for my CT scan I broke down. At the time I thought it was the pain of the dye going into my arm for the scan but, on reflection, I now know it was something much deeper than this. You see, this was the first time I had been alone since my diagnosis and I think what actually caused this reaction wasn't the physical pain but the emotional reality taking hold as I realised that I was embarking on a long journey in which, often, only medical staff would be able to hold my hand. I realised in that moment that my loved ones, as incredibly supportive as they were, could not walk this journey with me. They could cheer and support me from the sidelines of course, but there would be moments like this where I would be completely alone. In these moments the comfort they provided would come from the memory of their words rather than the warmth of their touch.

Just hours later (although it felt like years) my husband and I met with two surgeons to receive the preliminary results of my scan. They were informative and clear, recognising and accepting my need for information about my body. This gave me great comfort. I felt confident that I was in safe hands.

They explained that when looking at scan results they review the suspected primary sites first (in my case the ovaries) and then the vital organs (brain, liver and lungs) and then the rest. While we wouldn't get the full results until the following day they wanted to let us know that it had been confirmed that I had cancer in my ovaries and throughout my abdomen but, more positively, that my head and liver were clear. It's incredible, and important, to note that even at times as life changing as a suspected late stage cancer diagnosis that there can still be moments of utter elation and joy.

The following day I received my full results. This time the surgeons were joined by an incredible woman who I was told would be my specialist nurse. I was to discover that she would be my main point of contact. Over the coming months if I had any questions or concerns she would be there for me to provide answers or, failing that, to connect me with someone who could. She was, without doubt, a lifeline in a swirling sea of uncertainty.

The surgeons delicately explained that my cancer had spread throughout my abdominal cavity. Drawing diagrams, they discussed body parts I'd never heard of including my 'omentum' (the fat layer in front of your abdominal organs) and my 'peritoneum' (the 'sack' that contains these organs). They clearly explained that the cancer had affected all of my abdominal organs. None of my organs, however, with the exception of my left ovary, had cancer in them. Instead, they explained that the cancer was sitting on the organs. This, I learnt, was some good news.

Then came the bombshell. I could see it in their faces before the words left their lips.

'Your scan shows fluid on your right lung.' The words hung in the air. I didn't know what this meant but I knew it wasn't good.

'We'll need to do further biopsies to determine if this fluid is cancerous or not.' They went on explaining further, but I was no longer listening.

'Cancer on my lungs?' I thought. This couldn't be happening. I identified myself as a runner. I need my lungs.

'What does this mean? What stage is my cancer?' I managed to ask.

'Well we won't know for certain until we get the biopsy results but if the fluid on your lungs is cancerous then your cancer is stage four. This means that we may not be able to do surgery.' Realisation hit me. I not only had advanced ovarian cancer, but it was likely inoperable. Their smiles and friendly faces didn't match their words. I felt confused. How could this be happening? I was only

30 years old. I had been healthy, hadn't I?

'What would surgery involve?' I asked, not yet sure if I wanted to hear the answer.

'Well,' they exchanged looks as if silently agreeing whether I was ready to hear their words, 'if you are approved, surgery would be extensive. The peritoneum would need to be stripped. To do this your internal organs would need to be moved out of the way. Your omentum would need to be removed and you'd also have a complete hysterectomy. Some other organs may also have to be removed and you would likely require a permanent colostomy bag afterwards.'

They went on to explain that surgery would involve a team of up to six specialist surgeons in an operation lasting at least eleven hours. Again the words were delivered with calm and gentle smiles. I laughed, the result of an annoying coping mechanism I've acquired.

'The operation is quite serious. You'd likely be in intensive care afterwards.' There it was again, reality, hanging on their every word.

They explained that I would also need chemotherapy and, because of the aggressive nature of my cancer, that they would be starting with chemotherapy straight away. They would then be repeating the CT scan after three rounds of chemotherapy before making a final decision about whether an operation was possible or not.

'Plans change all the time. Let's just see what happens,' they offered.

I realised then that the only way to get through this journey without entirely freaking out was by taking it one day at a time. Mindfulness was forcing its way into my life whether I liked it or not.

I was put in a wheelchair and taken for my lung biopsy straight away. It's as awful as it sounds. Using an ultrasound the doctor guided a large needle in between the ribs in my back and drew out the fluid. Having been provided with no pain relief prior to the procedure, I found it agonising. The doctor drew three vials of fluid, placed them in a clear plastic bag and handed them to me.

'That's you good to go back to the ward. Just hand these to the nurse when you get there.'

'Don't I need a chest x-ray?' I asked, baffled. The ward had explained that this was protocol due to a risk of my lung being punctured during the procedure.

'No. You'll be fine,' he said dismissively.

My husband wheeled me back to the gynaecology ward and I handed over the fluid samples. They were horrified. Not only was I, as suspected, meant to have had a chest x-ray but also I should have been given pain relief and 'under no circumstances' should I have been handed the samples. These were meant to have gone directly to the lab. However, despite their horror at the situation, I'd found it quite fascinating to have had the opportunity to look at the samples. At the very least it gave me a means to visualise my cancer. While it may not have been 'protocol' I actually think that this experience helped me to restore a sense of calm. You see, the fluid looked so 'normal'. Instead of having blind fear about the cancer in my body I had inadvertently come face to face with it. I had seen it with my own eyes and it wasn't nearly as frightening as what my imagination had been demonstrating to me. This gave me power. Most importantly, it normalised the situation and, in doing so, it removed my fear and gave me hope. Perhaps it would benefit more patients to face their cancer in this way. But then again, perhaps not everyone has the same morbid curiosity as me.

After that I was free to go home with my 'suitcase' of drugs, containing an overwhelming concoction of pain relief and anti-sickness medication. At the time it baffled me that in less than one week I went from working full time and on no medication to being on morphine daily and hardly able to move or do anything for myself. Now with a deeper understanding of the mind-body connection I wonder if I was a victim of the 'nocebo' effect. Simply put, the 'nocebo effect' is the opposite of the 'placebo effect'. While the placebo effect can help us to heal, the nocebo effect can cause our bodies to negatively react and decline in response to the external messages received by our brain that are telling us we are 'terminal'.

It was pure nirvana to leave the hospital. The little things in life that we can all be guilty of taking for granted really are all that matter when it comes to being happy. Seeing my two cats and three chickens (Bhuna, Tikka and Balti - yes I named them after curries but only because they would never become one!), sitting on my sofa and cuddling my husband while we watched TV in the privacy of our own home without an audience of medical professionals were the greatest gifts of all. These simple daily joys that I had mindlessly taken for granted for so long were now making my heart sing.

I realised then, as I lay in my husband's arms, that my cancer was a gift. Despite years of warning signs trying to wake me up to a life half-lived and entirely undervalued, it wasn't until now, having come face to face with the prospect of my own death, that I was finally listening. My eyes had been opened.

From that moment my cancer became my 'guru' and I was ready and willing to listen, to take back control of my health and to start living as I used the lessons that cancer had brought, to heal my life and return to wholeness.

CHAPTER 2: MAINTAINING CONTROL

Before I could even think about beginning the conventional treatment being offered to me (namely chemotherapy) the main focus, aside from establishing the stage of my cancer, was to determine its genetic properties and manage my symptoms.

Having already had a fluid biopsy taken from my right lung, the next phase of testing was to be a tissue biopsy of my cancer. This involved several small cuts being made into my abdomen while I was awake. Yes, it is as unpleasant as it sounds, however, I was highly sedated for the procedure and so I can recall very little except for chatting about my pet chickens with the doctor while she carefully cut my body.

The main reason for the tissue biopsy was to ascertain whether my cancer had been caused by a BRCA gene mutation, as when such a mutation is present it can increase the chances of a woman developing either breast or ovarian cancer or both. This was considered likely as it is rare for a young, pre-menopausal woman to develop ovarian cancer that is not caused by a genetic mutation. However, the results of the biopsy surprisingly showed that my cancer cells did not demonstrate evidence of this mutation. In fact, further testing demonstrated that my cancer was not caused by any genetic faults. This was despite my paternal grandmother passing away from ovarian cancer and two maternal aunts having had breast cancer. While this was an obvious relief for my family – I have two sisters and a niece who would have had a higher risk of developing cancer themselves had I had a genetic cancer – it meant that my options for treatment were significantly reduced. For instance, I was no longer eligible for a number of drug trials or follow up drugs that are routinely offered to 'BRCA patients' upon completion of chemotherapy.

When I met my oncologist for the results of all of these tests she gently explained that my cancer was incurable.

'The aim is to get your cancer into remission, but it may come back and then we will go through this process again', she explained. 'The biopsy of your lung confirmed your cancer is stage four B. We can treat your symptoms but we can not cure you.'

The words hung heavily in the air. In the space of three weeks I had been told I didn't have cancer, then that I did. I had been told my cancer was possibly inoperable and now I was being told it was stage four B and incurable. These words were followed by her further explanation that my cancer was also high grade and, as a result, highly aggressive.

What was I meant to do with this news?

In all honesty, it wasn't entirely unexpected. I'd been told from day one that they thought this was the case but that they needed to do more biopsies before they could be sure. These had now shown that, as predicted, there was cancerous fluid on, not in, my right lung.

So how did this affect me? Well, for one, my positivity took a blow from this news. I was a runner. At the time of my diagnosis, running was my one and only hobby. All I could think was 'but I need good lungs to exercise.' I was devastated.

It wasn't so much the 'cancer' news that hurt but the news that a part of my body, that I very much valued above most other parts, was now damaged. I felt like part of my identity was being stripped away from me.

However, life works in mysterious ways and, as a result, all of that changed when I had an inspirational conversation with a near stranger, and equally passionate exerciser, just two weeks later.

'What you need to do every day is put on your running clothes and go for a walk at the time you used to run,' he explained.

I thought this was crazy. I'd already packed my running gear away in boxes in acknowledgment that I would never need it again. But he went on, suggesting that the psychology of these actions have positive associations for me and that by doing this routine I would be doing something positive for myself.

Then he gave the best piece of advice I'd heard since my diagnosis. 'If you walk in your running clothes every day, one day you may manage a 30 second run or one day you may even manage longer. But you know what? You won't ever manage to run sitting in your house.'

So from then on, every morning I would put on my running shoes and I go for a walk round the block and, although it was tiring at first, it became the highlight of my day. It was precious time I had carved into my day just for me that enabled me to reclaim my sense of self, connect with nature and, above all, feel alive. Now, three years later, I still go for a three-mile walk every morning.

The most important thing you can do following a cancer diagnosis is to take control of your disease and take ownership of the decisions being made. While it was, of course, hard to hear that my cancer was stage four B, incurable and aggressive, knowing this allowed me to make informed decisions about my healthcare plan and how I spent my time.

I truly feel that one of the most valuable lessons from my journey has been to take total ownership of my health. I can only hope that in the future integrated, person-centred treatment of cancer patients will become the norm.

On a personal level I've found that while doctors were initially surprised by my calm and rational (and often emotionally detached) questioning, they also always appear refreshed by the opportunity to talk openly about my illness with me in a way in which I am made to feel welcomed as a contributor rather than a bystander. As soon as you are diagnosed with cancer everything you identified as being 'you' can begin to change. Not only can treatment change your physical appearance and abilities but, regrettably, the diagnosis itself can change people's perception of you. As you work your way through a system designed to 'fix' you it can become all too easy to become labelled as a patient. Your diagnosis can begin to define you. However, you have the power to retain your identity and in doing so, you have the choice to take back control.

I've spent the vast majority of my working life talking about and researching person-centred healthcare. In fact, my career, before cancer, centred around helping healthcare professionals recognise how to put their patient first and adapting their services and care plans to meet patient needs. I thought I had it sussed.

I was wrong.

Having now lived the patient experience for myself I realise that person-centred care isn't just about creating individually tailored care packages – although, of course, that's important. Person-centred care is actually much simpler. It's just about seeing the person behind the condition. It's about having compassion. It's about caring and, above all, it's about listening.

Understandably it can be hard for a medical professional to do this. They are often overtired and overworked and seeing countless patients every single day. Not to mention, if we are going to be painfully honest, it may get more than a little upsetting for staff if they are to become personally attached to every patient they treat in an oncology ward.

What does 'person-centred care' have to do with my cancer treatment? Well, I've shared this because I want to be clear that the patient (as well as the medical team) has a valuable role in maintaining his or her own identity. I know it's not easy and even I – who had previously worked in this field for years – slipped easily into the role of 'the patient' who was having things done to her rather than having an active part in her treatment. However, this didn't last long and soon I regained an active role in my treatment plan. As a result my medical team treated me with mindful and mutual respect. This, I believe, served to keep me positive during my journey and, based on the research by Dr Kelly Turner in her incredible book 'Radical Remissions', may be one of the fundamental reasons why I am still alive today.

Less than a week following my diagnosis I was readmitted to hospital to receive a series of tests required before chemotherapy could commence the following week. I also required a second abdominal drain because, despite having drained five litres previously, fluid had returned and I was now, once again, unable to eat due to the resulting pressure on my stomach.

However, this time the abdominal drain wasn't as straightforward. This time I knew what to expect. I knew that despite the injections of anaesthetic that I would feel the push of the knife as it cut through the layers of flesh and muscle. I knew that the anaesthetic wouldn't reach the innermost layers and that when the knife reached this point I would face a deep searing pain. I felt helpless and alone, having asked my husband to step outside to save him from seeing me like that.

I put headphones in my ears and let the soft flows of meditation chimes fill my mind as I tried to control my breathing. 'Come on, focus', I internally screamed, clearly far from a meditative state.

Unlike with my previous abdominal drain, where a nurse had held an ultrasound on my tummy while the consultant guided the knife and draining tube into my abdominal cavity, this procedure was much less clinical.

I'd already been sent to the ultrasound department to have the drain site marked with a large black cross and now a junior doctor was going to perform the incision.

'It's important that you don't move too much after the scan. We don't want the fluid to move and accidentally cut through a nerve or an artery' he explained.

I was terrified.

As I lay there the doctor made several attempts to cut through the layers to reach the fluid. Each time he inserted the drain, however, no fluid was found. He was missing the correct spot repeatedly. By this point, despite my best attempts at meditative breathing, I was writhing in pain. The observing young nurse took my hand in hers to reassure me.

'Don't do that. Don't connect with the patient. You can't do that in oncology,' came the doctor's warning.

I understood the underlying message of his words

loud and clear. 'She's going to die. Don't get attached to her' was what he was really saying.

I was horrified. Had he completely forgotten I was lying in the bed in front of him? Had he really disconnected from me that much? This was a junior doctor about to embark on a career as one of the next generation's medics. How could he possibly think that this was an acceptable standard? Had medical training removed all forms of care? Had he forgotten why he wanted to become a doctor in the first place?

The nurse looked at me and gave a rye smile. I turned to face the doctor and politely explained that I didn't want further attempts at the drain that evening.

I never received treatment from that doctor again. Each time I made an excuse. I wasn't willing to let someone touch my already failing body who, despite my beating heart, no longer viewed me as a person. In making this decision I was taking back control. I realised then that, despite the respect I hold for medical staff, sometimes they can still lack the purest substance known to promote life: hope. My life was in my hands and I was going to be in charge of what happened with it.

Since releasing the first edition of this book I have read 'This is Going to Hurt - Secret Diaries of a Junior Doctor' by Adam Kay and I now feel nothing but compassion for this man who I had previously resented beyond measure. What must this poor soul have endured during his training and medical experience to go from pursuing a medical career to help people, to wishing to remain so disconnected from his oncology patients? It appears, on reflection, that in that moment the system hadn't just failed me (the patient) but also him (the doctor).

Now, of course, don't get me wrong there have been countless times where I have received the most compassionate care imaginable and these are speckled throughout this book. For instance, during this early stay on the oncology ward I was subjected to over 20 blood tests in the space of two days. I became fearful of a nurse walking in my room because, despite their friendly manner, they were always inflicting pain. Having previously been a regular blood donor, I was now growing terrified at the prospect of having more needles put into my increasingly bruised body.

One morning, after another restless night I was more than a little grumpy when a nurse came into my room first thing.

'I don't want any more blood tests.' I declared before she even had a chance to say why she had come in. Without a word she turned on her heels and left the room, returning five minutes later with an ice-lolly.

'If you are going to act like a five year old then I am going to treat you like one.' She laughed tenderly as she handed me the treat.

I felt completely safe and supported by her warmth. Needless to say she got to do the blood tests she had planned.

For me it is this quality of care that makes all the

difference. I've learnt that when you're at your lowest, lower than you thought humanly possible, all that matters is the compassion of one human to another; the care; the time; and the consideration to show love to another spirit. I can only hope that more people will realise that this is the care that gets people through the hard times and helps them to heal in every sense of the word.

You, 'the patient', have the power to take back control of your health and life at any stage. It is your body and your care; don't let someone else hold the wheel. All that you need to do is change some false beliefs about how you should conform to the role of 'the patient'.

Top Tips - How to Maintain Your Personal Power

1. Ask for your appointment to be changed if you can't make it. Don't believe that you must work your precious life around your appointments. I have found that whenever I have been unable to attend an appointment that the staff have been more than willing to accommodate a change.

2. Ask questions. If you want to know something then ask. Don't just wait for information to be given to you. When I see my oncologist we huddle around her computer so she can show me the graphs of data about my results. She also, at my request, shows me my scans. I feel a part of my team rather than on the outside of it. This is possible for you too and you will most likely find that your team will be pleased to include you. In the words of my oncologist it is 'refreshing' to welcome this type of relationship.

3. Create a dialogue with your team and be willing to say no to treatment that you don't want. Know that you have the ultimate power over what is done to you and your body. I have turned down scans, infusions and the option of second line chemotherapy. At one stage I was even part of the discussion about the drug quantities used in the final dose of chemotherapy I received. If done in a respectful and informed (remember the point above about asking questions) manner then you will find that your team welcome your insight. Ultimately remember that everything that your medical team offer you is a recommendation, it is not an obligation.

4. Off the back of this, if your team is offering you something you don't want or that doesn't 'feel right' for you then it is important that you also ask for what does feel right. Treat your medical team as you would a colleague and you will find that you are treated with this equal respect in return. If what you want can't be provided by your medical team then explain where you will seek this additional care. For instance if you are using complementary therapies then include your medical team in this. Create a tribe of support in which everyone respects and knows about each other. Only then can you hope for an ultimate care plan. For instance, my oncologist had the name and details of my herbalist. This meant that she was able to ask informed questions about the herbal therapies I used and raise any concerns regarding drug contradictions. This, ultimately, ensured my safety.

5. Maintain your identity at every possible stage. Get dressed up nice for your treatment and appointments. Treat it as a meeting with a friend. This is your moment

for health and healing, so it is important to embrace it as you. Not only will this most likely make you feel better, but it will also help your team to get to know you as an individual rather than as a patient. I wore a knitted mermaid tail blanket while getting my chemotherapy infusions so my medical team certainly got to know the real me.

In case you are wondering if I ever got the abdominal drain that the doctor wasn't able to perform, yes I did. I had it done the following day while sedated for another procedure. To this day I still question why this hadn't been the original plan. Not only would it have saved me a lot of unnecessary pain and distress, it also would have saved the National Health Service money. This is a clear example of why it is always acceptable to question your healthcare plan and ensure that you are always comfortable with the care you are receiving. Remember, out of everyone in our whole beautiful planet, it is you who knows your body better than anyone else. Open yourself up to the possibility of being treated as an equal in discussions about your health, take back control and treat your team with respect and wonderful things will start to happen. I wish you the same relationship I have with each of the members of my incredible, integrated team.

PART TWO

TREATING THE SYMPTOMS

CHAPTER 3: A CHEMICAL SHIT STORM

Disclaimer - This section of the book serves as a brutally honest and frank account of my personal experience of chemotherapy treatment and some of the steps I took to help get me through it.

Before we delve into this topic, I wish to highlight that there are now countless variations of chemotherapy drugs on the market and that everyone reacts to them differently. During my treatment I witnessed people react so badly that they had to cease treatment, but I also saw people sail through as if they were being infused with water. Every single person is different and I in no way wish to put you off having chemotherapy. Whether or not you choose to have chemotherapy (or indeed any medical treatment) is a very personal choice and one that should not be made lightly. At the time of my diagnosis I was convinced that if I didn't start chemotherapy treatment immediately, I would drop down dead. I was told I was inoperable and incurable. I was turned away from drug trials. My options appeared limited and, as a result, I was terrified to turn down the one thing I was being offered and so I embraced chemotherapy as 'my only option'. However, having now done extensive research, experienced the treatment for myself and spent a lot of time reflecting on my personal views, I have chosen to decline second line chemotherapy. Second line chemotherapy is the name given to chemotherapy that is offered in the event of cancer returning following a period of remission. That is, in the event that the first chemotherapy did not work. It is often a different type or an altered dose of the original chemotherapy.

This is an opinion I have shared openly with my oncologist and, despite the fear that filled me as I explained my choice, she didn't turn her back on me but instead continued to keep me within her care in an informed and equal partnership.

February 3rd 2016

Nothing prepares you for chemotherapy. You read the paperwork, you hear the descriptions of what it will be like, you've seen the portrayals in the media and television but you have no idea what it will feel like in your body. For me it was brutal.

When the week came to start treatment I was excited. I know that sounds crazy and no, I'm not an idiot. I knew it was going to be a bit of a shit storm (sometimes literally!) but I liked the idea that the medics were actually going to be doing something rather than just poking me with needles as they had done for the past few weeks. I was about to start my treatment journey and I was ready and willing. Or so I thought.

It was just sixteen days since I'd been told I had cancer. I was on daily anti-sickness drugs and morphine. In the space of two weeks everything about my life had changed. I could no longer walk for more than five minutes and I had even been taken into hospital after I collapsed while trying to walk around the block. I needed a drip to get fluid and nutrients into my body as my abdominal swelling was still preventing me from eating. My skin had been punctured with over 30 needles; I'd had countless blood tests, two abdominal drains, a lung biopsy and a tissue sample taken – all while I'd been awake! Every day had been filled with medication, pain, tests, doctors and nurses and I desperately wanted to start moving through this stage.

My medical team explained that my chemotherapy cycles were twenty-one days long with my chemotherapy being administered on Day Three. This meant that every three weeks I would receive a dose of chemotherapy.

On Day One I would have blood tests to check my CA 125 levels (aka ovarian cancer marker levels) as well as my white blood count to see if my immune system was strong enough for chemotherapy. The latter was particularly important with each subsequent dose of chemotherapy as my immune system would weaken with each dose. I came to dread these blood tests as my veins became increasingly fragile from the chemotherapy treatment and, subsequently, it became a painful challenge to get blood from my body. To this day this remains an issue.

The results of the blood tests would determine whether or not my body was in a suitable state to receive chemotherapy. When they did the blood tests on Day One there would always be the possibility that my blood count wouldn't be high enough for my next dose of chemotherapy. If this were the case then the chemotherapy ward would call me to let me know. I never received that call and, by some miracle, I was able to receive every chemotherapy dose as planned.

On Day Two I would take ten steroid tablets at midnight in preparation for chemotherapy the next day when I would take another ten tablets at 7am. This meant that I had little sleep the night before receiving chemotherapy as not only was there little time between the steroid doses but their side effects would lead me to be 'wired' enough to clean the whole house rather than rest. As I received subsequent doses of chemotherapy and got accustomed to the patterns of side effects, Days One and Two would become the days I would try and spend lots of time with my family, knowing that in the following week I wouldn't be well enough for visitors. I also began to use the night before to fill our freezer with food and tidy our house so that minimal effort was required post treatment. This never worked however as, for reasons unknown to me, the only things I ever wanted to eat in the days that followed were spicy vegetable pakora and ice-lollies!

On Day Three I would receive my dose of chemotherapy. For those of you who haven't had chemotherapy, rest assured that the process of actual administration is fairly straightforward. For me, I would just be sat in a room alongside fellow cancer warriors all receiving various types of chemotherapy themselves. The staff were friendly and well informed and music would play softly in the background.

I would arrive in the hospital for 9.30am to have a cannula fitted before being given an infusion of anti-sickness medication and antihistamine as well as medication to protect my stomach lining. All of these were to help ensure that my body didn't reject the chemotherapy and subsequently make me extremely ill. 'Why would my body reject the chemotherapy?' you might be wondering. Well, while chemotherapy is extremely effective at destroying cancer cells it is also, subsequently, effective at destroying all fast growing cells within your body i.e. the cells in your skin and nails, stomach lining, intestines, immune system, bone marrow, reproductive organs and mouth (to name a few). It is basically a chemical substance that is attacking your body. As a result, pharmaceuticals have developed a number of medications to counteract the inevitable side effects. To check that these were working I would be monitored by the nursing staff during my chemotherapy infusion to ensure that at no point was I having a dangerous reaction. This included, for example, blood pressure and temperature checks. Administration of these drugs would take about 30 minutes for each one and involved a syringe to flush the cannula with saline between each drug. Because of the need for all of these medications it wouldn't be until around 11am that I would actually receive the start of my chemotherapy treatment.

At each chemotherapy appointment (every twenty-one days) I received two different chemotherapy drugs: Paclitaxol and Carboplatin. I also received a maintenance drug called Bevacizumab (more commonly known as Avastin) that is proven to help prevent cancer cells from growing new blood vessels. As a result, every three weeks, I would spend eight hours in the 'chemo day unit' hooked up to an IV. Many chemotherapy treatments, however, take much less time and over the course of my six months of chemotherapy I became used to people arriving after me and leaving before me, requiring only an hour or two of treatment.

These drugs were all administered through an IV into the cannula in my hand, starting with Paclitaxol which took around three hours. Upon completion a nurse would 'flush the line'. This involved running a glucose solution through my cannula in the same way that the chemotherapy had done. This was to prevent the next type of chemotherapy drug mixing with this one in the line. I was informed that the reason glucose was used instead of saline was because the chemotherapy could react to a saline solution. I can't say I was ever thrilled to have glucose fed into my body in this way, especially as I had given up sugar as part of my anti-cancer protocol (more on this in Part Four).

The next chemotherapy drug I would receive was Carboplatin. This was administered over 90 minutes and then, again, followed by another glucose flush through my cannula. Finally I would receive the Avastin, another flush of glucose and, after sitting for half an hour to ensure no delayed reaction, I would finally be able to return home.

All went well in the hospital during my first dose. I sat with my husband by my side and we switched from chatting to reading to watching films. There were no side effects at this stage and, aside from being slightly bored, there was nothing to complain about.

Nothing prepared me, however, for the torture that would ensue once I returned home.

There is a long list of potential side effects ranging from bladder and bowel issues to hair loss, sickness, insomnia, fatigue, loss of feeling in hands and feet, pain and so on. The list seemed endless. Following a chemo dose I would be given a card listing them all and asked to rate each of my own symptoms on a scale of 0-3 each day for the next three weeks. If, at any stage, any of my symptoms reached a score of 2 or 3 (i.e. moderate or severe) then I was told to call a specialist cancer care line for help.

All that said, I am very pleased to report that I didn't get hit with every potential side effect. Instead, my experience can best be described as a mixture of your worst hangover ever, while you have the flu and food poisoning and trying to do an insane workout in the gym. Yes, it really was that bad!

Just two hours after I was home I was throwing up constantly. It was horrendous! This lasted for four days with times where I just put a towel on the bathroom floor so that I could have a nap in between being sick and soiling myself. It is honestly a sickness like no other. I can't put into words how weak and tired I began to feel. It was like my bones were breaking. My legs, ribs and jaw screamed in pain. I would spend my time moving between the sofa and the bathroom waiting desperately for night to come so I could go to bed and escape the torture. When night arrived, however, I wouldn't be able to sleep. Instead I would toss and turn as my body screamed internally. This, I now know, was a result of the chemo destroying my bone marrow while also removing my body's ability to absorb sufficient magnesium from external sources resulting in Hypomagnesemia - a long term electrolyte disturbance I now endure to this day, as a result of the low levels of magnesium in my blood and an inability for my body to effectively absorb magnesium from external sources. I would lie there willing the sun to come up, hopeful of a better day. However, when morning would eventually arrive, after what felt like an eternity of torture, the same issues would ensue and the cycle would continue. I longed for the end of side effects. During these moments of darkness I would take comfort in reminding myself that I was doing it for the people I love. However, the more I researched the more I began to question whether the damage that chemo was causing my healthy cells and my already weakened body was, in reality, worth it.

Thankfully, for me, the periods of debilitating side effects only lasted for around a week. Following that I would have two weeks where I would feel more myself, able to leave the house and enjoy my life, although a little slower than before. Following those two weeks I would receive another dose and the cycle would continue again. The worst part was that I always knew that I had another dose to receive. Each time I always had a mixture of emotions ranging from excitement that my cancer would be receiving another hit, to dread at the prospect of the onslaught of the subsequent side effects. I would just be starting to feel normal again with my body recovering from the damage chemotherapy was doing, when I would have to start all over again. Each time the effects would hit me harder as my body grew increasingly damaged by the toxicity of the high dose chemotherapy I was receiving.

In the days following my chemotherapy I would continue to take steroids as well as medication to prevent damage to my stomach. As I swallowed each tablet I would question my treatment, wondering how something that was meant to be helping me could be doing so much damage to my body.

Life with Fatigue

The fatigue that I felt as a result of the long-term damage that chemotherapy did to my body and my subsequent Hypomagnesemia is so hard to describe. We are talking out of breath from having a shower; needing to sit down after doing the food shopping; unable to clean your own house.

Sleep didn't elevate it. As time passed and I received subsequent doses it became challenging to get my brain and body to function as one, as I became increasingly plagued by fatigue. I could be lying on the sofa wanting a glass of water. I'd think about getting the glass of water and even drinking the water. However, the actual act of getting myself off the sofa to get the glass of water would take about an hour for my brain to process.

Now let's get one thing straight, fatigue and tiredness are not the same thing. Not even close. You don't know what fatigue is like until you've experienced it. I don't care how many kids you have, how many late nights you've had, how hungover you are, what your work pattern is (insert anything else here) you just don't! Yeah I thought I knew what it was before too but it turns out I was wrong.

Fatigue is like waking up each day with four cups of energy while everyone else has twenty. You can choose how you spend each cup. You might choose to use two on seeing a friend, one on yoga and one on cooking dinner. The rest of the time would be spent lying down. So each day is about making a decision on where to spend your cups. Also keep in mind that obviously sometimes you have to spend cups on doing housework, paperwork, food shopping and other necessities. In amongst all of this I also needed to find the energy to spend time with my husband - sleeping with my head on his shoulder while he watches TV doesn't count as quality time - and with my incredible family.

But, now pay attention, you can't spend five cups one day and expect it to be okay because you'll just have three the next day. That is how tiredness works. That is not how fatigue works. With fatigue if you spend five cups instead of four then it will cost you all of the cups for the next couple of days. In my case this would manifest in sickness, sleeping and an inability to think and function clearly.

Personally I choose to spend my cups on yoga and writing because I am extremely passionate about them and I want to make a difference for others. The days I don't do either of those things I feel lost. They are what make my heart sing and if cancer has taught me anything it's to do what matters most to you with the time you have.

When you start to add all these things together you soon see that the four cups of energy don't spread far. Especially when, in the analogy, a 'normal' person has about five times as many cups each day and they can 'borrow' from other days too.

This meant that during the months I was receiving my chemotherapy treatment, and for over a year afterwards, I had to carefully plan when I would use cups on social activities. Don't get me wrong, I would love to have maintained the same ability to socialise that I had before cancer but it just wasn't an option for me.

Fatigue is a really disabling condition and it's also emotionally challenging because sometimes the people you care about, as hard as you might try to explain, just don't get it. As a result I became increasingly reliant on my husband for support. So, if you are going through your own journey with fatigue, know that you are not alone. I get it and, maybe, one day others will too.

Hair Loss

Prior to starting treatment I was told that I would lose my hair. In a bid to maintain control I made a pledge to cut off my long blonde hair the night before I started my chemotherapy and donate it to 'The Little Princess Trust', to be used in a wig for a child facing cancer. This could have been a really depressing night, but, thanks to the support of the people I love, it was a fun night full of laughter and happy memories. In fact, each member of my family had a turn in cutting off some of my hair alongside the hairdresser. This empowered me and gave me hope that my hair was going to a great cause rather than being lost as a result of treatment. I had my remaining short hair dyed pink and purple to raise money for charity. Already, in these early days, I was striving for positives to come from my diagnosis.

The best part was other people started to cut off and donate their hair too, or dye their hair similar shades of pink. The Little Princess Trust received countless donations as a result and so much money was raised for Macmillan that I would later be awarded Scottish Volunteer Fundraiser of the Year and win a Macmillan Award. All this happened just because I had been diagnosed with cancer and I was driven to ensure that many more positives would arise as a result.

If you are going to lose your hair as a result of chemotherapy then I encourage you to maintain control and cut it short beforehand. Buy a wig you love (some charities will fund this for you) or treat yourself to some headscarves that coordinate with your wardrobe. If your hair is long enough (you will need a ponytail measuring at least seven inches) then you can donate it and know that, because of you, a child will get to have hair while they go through their own cancer treatment.

Five weeks later I started losing my hair in clumps. Especially when I was in the shower or bath. I thought I would find this much more distressing than I actually did. In reality, it's not as bad as you think it's going to be. It may be that by the time your hair starts falling out you have dealt with so much that it pales in comparison but it didn't really bother me at all. This was unexpected. I'd always considered myself to be vain but, once again, I was surprising myself with my strength as I faced this journey and embraced the spirit I'd found buried deep within.

After a couple of weeks there was no denying that my hair was not going to stop falling out. So I took the plunge and asked my wonderful husband to shave my head completely. It was so empowering. Rather than feeling sad or embarrassed, I stood in front of the mirror and embraced the warrior who stood before me. She was strong and powerful and looked capable of anything. Shaving my head felt like I was taking control and, although a drastic change, I was actually okay with it.

For so many years I had stressed, like many women, about bad hair days yet here I was embracing no hair at all and I still felt incredibly sexy.

I never wore my wig. For me it made me feel like I was trying to hide the fact that I had cancer, like it was something to be ashamed of. I hated the way that thought made me feel. So instead I started to play around with headscarves. I'm sure I spent an absolute fortune trying different combinations! The best part about wearing these is that you have a whole new accessory to coordinate with your outfits! I love when outfits are based around a colour and so I actually found this a fun process when getting ready in the morning.

One day I made the decision to embrace my beautiful bald head and went out with no headscarf for all the world to see. And do you know what happened? Nothing! No one gave a single fuck! It turns out that strangers don't really care what other strangers look like - even if they have no hair! Who'd have thought it, after years of worrying what other people thought about me, it turns out they are too busy worrying the same thing to even notice. Isn't that refreshing.

Infertility

After hearing the words 'you have late stage cancer' you don't think there is much worse news your doctors could drop on you. Sadly there is.

The day following my diagnosis I was destined to hear a number of unsavoury statements: 'The chemo will likely make you infertile'; 'Your cancer is too late stage and aggressive to preserve your eggs'; 'Chemo will likely put you through an early Menopause'; 'You have a hormone dependent cancer so you won't be able to take HRT'; 'Even if chemo doesn't make you infertile, surgery would involve a complete hysterectomy.'

In short, I was being told, 'You will never, ever have children'.

The news took a while for me to come to terms with. I was already grieving the loss of a child and, with it, the loss of a future that was entirely different from the one I was destined to face. Now my future was changing even more. However, I have since healed these wounds. With time, I have come to terms with the news and I have now reached the point where I can write about my experience in the hope of helping others to understand what it feels like, and to support those who are walking the same journey.

Reflecting on my emotions during this time I now offer you some Dos and Don'ts for supporting someone who has either lost a child or, after years of hoping to become a parent has found out they are infertile.

Don't:

1. Say you know how they feel. Even if you have gone through similar you don't know how *they* feel. You know how *you* felt. Let them tell you how they feel.

2. Complain about pregnancy. Whatever your symptoms, however bad they get, your friend would trade places with you in a heartbeat. Talk about how you are feeling of course but never complain. You get to hold your baby at the end of it. Always remember that.

3. Ignore their loss. If a friend has shared that they have experienced a loss or infertility don't ignore it, instead see the 'do' section below.

4. Feel you can't share your pregnancy/baby joy with them. Everyone may be different but, personally, I love hearing my loved ones are pregnant or when a new baby arrives. It provides joy and hope and love. Don't ever presume that someone who can't have children (or has lost a child) won't want to be part of your happiness. By 'protecting' them from this you will only make them feel more sad and isolated. Some of my favourite friends are those who still invite my hubby and me to their little one's birthday parties.

Do:

1. Tell your friend you love them and that you are there for them. Then actually make sure you are. Ask what you can do to help. Be their shoulder to cry on.

2. Acknowledge your friend was pregnant. Only two friends ever asked me how I'd found my pregnancy symptoms. Was I sick? Tired? Excited? Scared? This acknowledgment made a massive difference to me.

3. Share your personal stories. While you shouldn't say 'I know how you feel' your friend may find comfort in hearing that you have had a similar experience. I certainly appreciated when friends felt they were able to share their personal stories and let me know how they had felt without assuming I felt the same. This has built valued friendships and support.

4. Remember pregnancy loss and infertility affects men too. So many people would ask my hubby how I was without acknowledging that he had lost a child and wouldn't be able to have children as a result of my diagnosis too.

Top Tips - How to Cope Better with Chemotherapy

As brutal as chemotherapy treatment is, and as painful as some of the consequences can be, there is so much that you can do to make the process easier. During my treatment I received high doses of not one, but two, different types of chemotherapy over a six month period in which I also had extensive surgery. To say that I've learnt a few 'tricks of the trade' would be an understatement.

I've shared them here not as a strict protocol for you to follow, but rather to offer guidance and hope and to let you know that you are not alone and that, inevitably, there is light at the end of the tunnel.

1. Drink plenty of water. This is probably the most important tip I can offer. Following chemotherapy your body is filled with toxins that will put a strain on your already weakened immune system. It is these toxins that lead to many of the unwanted side effects commonly associated with cancer treatment. By simply drinking at least two litres of water on the day you receive chemotherapy and the three days after, you will be saving your kidneys and liver a lot of stress and hard work. Drinking tea and coffee is not the same and neither, unfortunately, is drinking alcohol or any kind of fizzy drink. Just drink plain water and enjoy the benefits. Trust me, your body will thank you for it.

2. Keep a list detailing your medication and emergency telephone numbers with you at all times. In the event of having to phone the hospital out of hours, the first thing they will ask you is what medication you are on. It saves a lot of stress and anxiety to have this information to hand in an emergency. It may also be helpful that key friends and family members have this information too in case you are out with them and they need to make a call on your behalf. If you are like me, and fiercely independent, then this idea may horrify you. For me, I liked to view it that I was 'project managing' my treatment and emergency care plan. I was still in control but just covering all eventualities. Trust me, from experience of trying to remember what medication I was on while writhing in pain, a pre-made list is much more sensible.

3. Don't suffer in silence. If you are struggling with side effects then phone the hospital for help. They have an array of medication to combat every known side effect to chemotherapy and, as a result, they can help you feel much better in moments. If you have any doubts, anxieties or are unable to cope with the sides effects then just pick up the phone. It is what they are there for and, in their words, they would much rather a phone call than an emergency admission because you tried to be a hero.

4. Get plenty of rest. Your body has just been filled with chemicals designed to attack and kill all fast growing cells, including many of your good ones and, as a result, you will naturally feel tired and fatigued. This is perfectly normal and not something you should give yourself a hard time over. It gets easier a few days following chemo and before you know it you will be back to normal. In the meantime, the ironing and housework can wait. Take the opportunity to rest on your sofa, read a book or watch some TV. Give your body the best chance to heal by taking some time out from your busy schedule. This may also mean you don't have the energy to see lots of visitors. That's okay too. I found conversations, and even replying to online messages, exhausting in the days following treatment. It's okay to be a little selfish (as long as you aren't mean) and put off seeing other people until you are well enough. Remember, your health comes first.

5. Relaxation is so important when going through

cancer treatment. Unlike rest, relaxation is more about your mind than your body. It is perfectly natural for your mind to be racing at 100 miles an hour with all of the information, worries and thoughts now filling it. However, it is fundamental to your health that you allow your mind a chance to let these thoughts go. In doing so you can begin to build on positive thoughts and emotions and continue to enjoy life as you go through your journey. There are many ways to do this. For me yoga and meditation were a huge help, as was practicing daily gratitude. There are now countless apps that guide you through meditation if you are new to it. Or you can simply just find a quiet place to focus on your breathing and let your thoughts go. Massage is also great; however always check with your medical team about whether this is a safe option for you. I know for me that I am no longer able to have my torso massaged and instead choose head and neck massage, foot and leg or hand massage. I also treat myself to the occasional facial. All of these are great ways to let your mind 'switch off'. The first massage I had following my diagnosis was an emotional experience for me. It wasn't until the massage started that I realised that for the previous three months I had been touched by so many strangers, each of whom were inflicting pain and anxiety. I had been examined, scanned (MRI, CT and ultrasound), had blood tests, fluid drained for my abdomen (twice), fluid biopsies taken from my lung and tissue biopsies taken from my abdomen. I'd had multiple IVs for fluid and chemotherapy and I'd also had two blood transfusions. It was during that first massage, however, that I realised I was now being touched in a way that was nurturing and caring. The massage was about my emotional wellbeing, rather than physical testing, and this enabled me to regain some power within my body and over my treatment. Since then I have had regular massages to help balance the emotions felt when having invasive, and often painful, treatment.

I've learnt through experience that having an anxious mind can also make receiving treatment harder than it might need to be. When we are anxious our bodies go into 'fight or flight' mode. This causes our blood to rush to our internal organs making it harder for a nurse to get access to a vein for treatment. It also stimulates our pain receptors, making things seem more painful than they actually are. I was very lucky to have an incredible chemotherapy nurse who recognised this and would sing to me while she was trying to put a needle into my hand. It worked every time because she got me to laugh and helped my mind to relax. A simple way to do this for yourself without bursting into song is just to breathe in for a count of two and breathe out for a count of four.

6. Food and diet play a huge role in ensuring that you are strong enough to receive subsequent doses of chemotherapy. It is normal for chemotherapy to affect your appetite and change your sense of taste. It can also cause mouth ulcers and a feeling of nausea. As a result, eating may not be at the top of your 'to do' list. However, if you are to remain strong and help your body recover then it is essential that you get yourself eating little and often. For me it really helped to do my food shopping the day before chemotherapy and make a few meals that I could pop in the freezer. This meant that in the days following treatment I had to give food little thought as it was already made. I also bought lots of healthy, high calorie snacks like avocados, dried fruit and nuts so that even if I wasn't eating very much I knew that what I was eating was doing my body good. Weight loss is common when having chemotherapy treatment but it is also a red flag to hospital staff. So even if meals aren't happening for you then learn how to make some high calorie smoothies and snacks. For instance, blending an avocado, a banana, a handful of almonds, some raw cacao with some water creates a healthy 'chocolate milkshake' that is easy to make, easy to eat and fuels your body quickly. It also tastes delicious too!

7. Exercise and time in nature are proven to reduce the side effects of cancer treatment as well as aiding recovery time. While you may feel tired and the thought of moving from your couch/bed/floor may be far from your mind it does help. Trust me! When I started chemotherapy treatment I couldn't walk around the block without collapsing and requiring an emergency hospital admission. Two months later, however, I was walking two or three miles a day. On the days following chemotherapy I wouldn't walk as far but I would still make myself leave the house and get some fresh air during a short walk. Yoga became a massive part of my life too during my recovery and ever since. I even trained to become a yoga teacher.

I never went to a gym for exercise. Firstly they are full of other people sweating and as chemotherapy lowers your immune system it wasn't a risk I was willing to take. Secondly, why pay for a gym when you can spend time outside and get some healthy vitamin D for free? I love time in nature. It always makes me feel so relaxed and calm and, dare I say it, healthy. This is such a priceless feeling when you are chronically (and even critically) sick.

Spending time in nature forces you to simply be in the moment. It is a powerful and precious experience and if you take nothing else from my book then please just step outside and breathe in the healing beauty of nature, or at the very least buy a house plant and open a window wide. Breathe.

8. Always be prepared. I would always pack my 'chemo survival kit' the night before treatment. I would take a couple of books to read, an adult colouring book (because, let's face it, they are super relaxing), a tablet loaded with things to watch, headphones, an extra long charging cable to ensure I could reach a plug, a blanket and cozy socks or slippers. I also made sure I was dressed in comfy clothes with lots of layers. During treatment I could go from feeling roasting hot to freezing cold and back again in a matter of minutes. Layers of clothing helped to ensure I was able to remove or add clothes accordingly. On a more practical level I would always take my diary (I'm old-school and like a paper planner) and notebook so that I could write down anything that was said to me. I also took food with me because, let's be honest, hospital food is awful and has the same nutrient value as eating paper.

I kept an overnight hospital bag packed and ready to go in case of an emergency. During my first year with cancer I had four unplanned hospitals admissions, one of which was via a 'blue light' ambulance. Having a bag packed already with everything I would need for a couple of days gave me a lot of peace of mind and meant that in an emergency my hubby wasn't rushing around the house looking for various items. That said, I have now unpacked that bag and what a joy it was realising how far

I had come that I was no longer at 'high risk' of an unplanned admission.

9. Get up, shower and put on some clean clothes. No matter how rubbish you feel always, always, always, get out of bed and have a shower or a bath even if only to put back on your pyjamas afterwards. You will always feel much better afterwards. When I was having chemotherapy I used to spend hours in the bath or shower. Although, in honesty, sometimes I'd spend so long in the bath because just the thought of getting out of the bath was exhausting. Instead I would just keep refilling the tub with hot water. There was something so mesmerising and therapeutic about the sound of running water when your brain has been numb from chemotherapy. Afterwards, exhausted, I would put on clean pyjamas and bed down on the couch feeling tired but much more refreshed. I also always made a point of doing my makeup even if just to lie about the house and especially on the days I went to hospital for treatment. Not only did it help me to feel more like myself, especially considering I had lost my hair and over two stone in weight, but it also helped medical staff to see 'me' rather than a sick cancer patient. Nothing made me feel more sorry for myself than looking at my grey bare face in the mirror. A simple stroke of blusher and bronzer, however, and I felt much better.

10. Make connections with other people who are going through cancer and cancer treatment. Cancer can be lonely. Your friends and family and loved ones are all there supporting you and cheering you on but, fortunately/hopefully, none know what you are going through. None feel your pain. None feel your worry as your worst fears crowd your mind. Instead they can just hold your hand, tell you they love you and watch (and cheer) from the sidelines.

Fellow cancer warriors are different. They have felt your pain. They have breathed your fears. They know the pain of telling loved ones their diagnosis; of hearing a medical professional put a timeframe on their lives; of having their lives change forever in a single breath. They are on the same journey.

Making connections, either online or face to face, with other people going through similar is a great way to support yourself and others through the experience.

A great way to meet people is in the chemotherapy room. For this reason I started going to my chemo sessions alone so that I could connect with other people in a more natural way. There is nothing like a healthy person sitting next to you while you are hooked up to tubes and machines with chemotherapy running through your veins to invite the 'pity party'. Not for me thank you!

I am so glad that I made this decision because, as a result, I met some incredible people and had some heart-warming conversations that I don't think I'd have embraced so freely in the company of a healthy supporter. This was what my soul needed at that time. I needed to connect with people who knew what it felt like to live with cancer and go through treatment. We were on the same journey and we were able to laugh and joke together. Yes, it's okay to joke and laugh in a chemo room. It doesn't have to be all doom and gloom. As with life, receiving chemotherapy (or any other treatment) is what you make it.

On this life-changing journey I met inspiring people, who not only helped me through my treatment but who also change the way I see the world and the way I see myself. I have been blessed to meet many wonderful people. Some are healthcare professionals, some are volunteers and some are fellow warriors. We walk this journey together, guiding one another. I would have been lost without them.

11. Practicing gratitude is one of the best things you can do for your mental health. Yes I know gratitude may be the furthest thing from your mind when going through cancer treatment but, in reality, you still have so much to be grateful for. Yes you've been diagnosed with cancer and that is a bit shitty but let's all pick ourselves up for a minute and remember all the people that are helping us to get through this. We have our amazing loved ones for instance who go above and beyond to help us. We also have our amazing medical teams (whether conventional, complementary or both) who are working tirelessly to enable us to heal. How wonderful it is that there is so much research available that enables us to progress every day on our chosen treatment journey.

CHAPTER 4: CUT TO PIECES

Early May 2016

When I was first diagnosed I was told that my cancer was likely inoperable because it was not only detected throughout my abdomen, but it was also evident on my right lung. When a cancer warrior is approved for surgery it is because the specialist team of surgeons believe that they will be able to remove all evidence of the disease and therefore the benefits of the surgery outweigh the risk. In my case, however, at the time of my diagnosis, they carefully explained that it would be too high a risk to operate on my abdomen and chest cavity at the same time and thus they wouldn't be able to remove all of my cancer in one operation. This decision is common with stage four cancer warriors, not least because our bodies are already so weak and struggling to survive without the additional assault of major surgery.

When I heard this news, however, I didn't lose hope. Instead I asked the team to carefully describe what the surgery would involve if I were to be approved. I also asked what would need to happen within my body for surgery to become a viable option.

'Your lungs would need to be clear and the cancer within your abdomen would need to appear significantly smaller at your next scan.'

So, that became my main focus. I needed to get my lungs healthy and clear of cancer and I needed to get my body fit enough for the possibility (however small) of having surgery.

In addition to the conventional treatment I was having I used a variety of complementary therapies to help my body to heal (for differentiation and clarity these are detailed in Part Four of this book). Over the next couple of months I had regular blood tests to check whether my cancer marker levels where reducing in response to this integrated approach to healing. The results were unbelievable. Just six weeks after I was diagnosed I received the exciting news that my markers were indeed decreasing. At the time I didn't want to get too excited, instead believing that the NHS wouldn't have spent thousands of pounds on my chemotherapy if this result hadn't been entirely expected. However, I have since discovered that while this result was 'hoped' for, it was by no means a certainty due to the advanced spread of my cancer. This is a reality that, sadly, I now hear all too often within the online cancer communities in which I connect with fellow late stage warriors.

In response to this result, I was scheduled to have a CT scan four weeks later so that the medical team could see what my cancer was doing in comparison to the scan they had taken at the time of my diagnosis. Two weeks following the scan, I received the news I had been hoping for. My results had been better than expected. My lungs were completely free from evidence of cancer. Against the odds, the surgeons all agreed that I was in the position where they could successfully remove all evidence of disease during one operation. They were going to operate. I couldn't believe my ears! It was just 12 weeks since I'd been diagnosed!

In that moment, and many moments since, I came to realise that the situation can change at any given point. No matter how dire the prognosis or situation there is still the possibility that it will all change for the better. I now fully appreciate the value of living in the moment and embracing today without fear for tomorrow. Above all, I have learnt that where there is breath, there is hope. I think all too often medical professionals want us to be 'realistic' about our diagnosis for fear that we aren't taking it seriously enough. Now, don't get me wrong, I am fully respectful of this. I know how dire my prognosis is. However, I question what benefit this brings to a patient in their final years, months or even days. From the moment we start to believe in our minds that we are dying, our bodies start to respond. In her book 'Mind Over Medicine', Dr Lissa Rankin discusses evidence of cases where patients where misdiagnosed as having cancer when, in fact, they did not. Some of the patients believed this fact so much that their bodies shut down and they died. They died of shock; they died from the very belief that they had cancer. Remember, these were perfectly healthy people with no scientific reason for their death. In short, there was no evidence of cancer in their body.

Recently I met a loving group of young women who were marking the passing of one of their dear friends. 'She was so positive through her cancer treatment until the moment she was given a time frame,' they explained to me. 'As soon as she was told she was going to die she did.' Now, I'm not suggesting that patients shouldn't be told when their prognosis is poor. After all, I always want to know everything about my situation. What I am suggesting, however, is that the medical professionals who care for people with a poor prognosis, should take caution of how this information is delivered. It is possible to deliver this information with love and even, in some cases, with humour. Working together as a team, isn't it better that both the patient and their medical team strive for an outlook that is both realistic and positive at the same time? After all, in the words of one member of my medical team 'you're not dead yet!'

Before I even had a moment to process the news that I had been approved for surgery, I was sitting with my oncologist, specialist nurse and a surgeon, who were giving me a clear and detailed explanation of what the surgery would involve, the recovery time, the risks and the long-term implications. They were thorough and, once again, I felt completely involved in my treatment plan as they explained that the scans showed that my cancer had shrunk in all areas of my body and at a rate faster than they had expected. They explained that they would be performing 'major' surgery.

I still vividly remember how the simple addition of the word 'major' filled my already buzzing head with a million new thoughts and questions. Because their ultimate aim was to remove as much cancer as they could, they explained that a specialist team of surgeons would perform the operation over a period of about eleven hours during which they would remove everything they could. They went on to explain that the extent of the surgery planned meant that I would need to spend some time in intensive care and/or high dependency. It also meant that potentially I would be in hospital for up to a month receiving specialist care. As if all of that hadn't been enough to process, they dropped a final bombshell; the operation would take place in another hospital, two hours from my home.

I felt completely overwhelmed. It was amazing, surprising and terrifying news and, as a result, I had very mixed emotions in the two weeks between hearing that I had been approved for surgery and going for my actual operation.

Having been originally told that my cancer was likely inoperable, I knew all too well how devastating it is to hear that surgery isn't an option. I couldn't help but think of the many people with cancer who would never meet a surgeon or have the opportunity to have their cancer removed. As a result I was, of course, filled with gratitude for the blessing and opportunity not only to have been approved for surgery but also to have access to free healthcare - a luxury denied by many on a similar journey. However, in the same breath I was absolutely terrified that I would not survive surgery and that, if I did, the associated risks and recovery would be too much for my already frail body. Aside from the fact that the last time I'd had surgery my heart had stopped due to a suspected reaction to anaesthetic, there were countless other risks now facing me. Thinking these thoughts I would become overwhelmed with guilt knowing that so many people would swap places with me in a heartbeat just to have the opportunity to have their cancer removed, whatever the risk.

To get myself through this I spoke endlessly with family and friends. Obviously they all wanted me to have the surgery but I was relieved that they listened to my fears and comforted me. Ultimately, however, the decision had to come from me and I knew that I needed to be completely comfortable with the prospect of surgery if I was to be emotionally strong enough to recover afterwards. With this in mind it was essential that I knew all of the risks associated with my operation. While I appreciate this may not be helpful for everyone, for me it was about appropriately preparing myself both physically and emotionally.

Obviously facing major surgery doesn't come without risk and in a meeting with my lead surgeon she explained all of the complications she could potentially face during my operation. One such example was that my lung could puncture while they worked on my diaphragm. This, they explained would result in me waking with a tube in my lung. Although this may sound scary, I was told, it is something that the human body is capable of repairing itself over time.

She explained that I may require blood transfusions during the operation or that I may wake up with a colostomy bag as a result of them removing part of my bowel. She also explained that they may open me up to discover that the scan had not given an accurate indication of the cancer in my body and that they would not be able to perform the operation safely. In this instance they would 'stitch me back up' without removing anything. This, in honesty, was a more terrifying prospect than the surgery itself. The thought of going through all of it for nothing was awful.

I continued to ask questions until I was satisfied that the surgeon was telling me everything. This moment came when she explained that she would need to work around some major arteries. 'What risk does that pose?' I asked naively. 'Well,' she started delicately, 'if you haemorrhaged we wouldn't be able to do anything.' I heard her loud and clear. This surgery came with the ultimate risk. There was a risk that I might not survive it. I could die on the operating table.

Oddly, this gave me the confidence I needed to sign the consent form permitting the surgery. While I had, in all honesty, spent the previous weeks wondering whether surgery was the right option for me, her honesty gave me reassurance. Yes she was telling me the worse news possible - news that this surgery was, in itself, life threatening - but her confidence and honesty to do so led me to believe that not only would she do her utmost to ensure that this didn't happen but that she respected me as an equal part in the decision. I felt in safe hands.

Top Tips - How to Stay Informed Prior to Surgery

Facing the prospect of any type of surgery is daunting and whether it is routine or major there are always risks to weigh up against the benefits. Throughout my journey it was important to me to remain in complete control of my healthcare plan and everything it entailed. This meant that I always wanted (and still want) to know everything. While I appreciate that when we become a 'patient' we are not always ready to hear everything, the 'researcher' within me treated this whole process like a living, breathing research study. If I were to embrace this wholeheartedly, with the aim of giving my body the best possible chance of recovery, then I would need to know what my medical team knew. We needed to be a team. How else would I be able to make informed decisions about my care?

If you are facing surgery, or supporting a loved one through this phase in their journey then I encourage you to ask questions. Yes, sometimes we hear scary stuff but we might also hear stuff that is much better than the terrifying thoughts our imagination can sometimes feed us. Above all, whatever we are told only serves to help us maintain control over our health and this is the key to healing.

The questions we will each want to ask are entirely personal. Not only does our individual diagnosis determine what is relevant to ask but so does our individual lifestyle and personality. However, I have listed the questions I asked as a reference to help you get started. My advice would be to write down your own questions and take them with you whenever you have an appointment with your medical team. This ensures that you won't forget them in the moment. I still do this now, as I am constantly learning about my diagnosis and my recovery. My only advice would be to always reflect on your questions to see if they come from a place of fear or a place of knowledge and enquiry. Through experience it is always better to ask questions with the intention of informing yourself and helping yourself to heal rather than trying to alleviate fears. If you are asking your medical team to be honest with you, then you need to be prepared for the answers.

I have listed some examples to get you started.

General Questions

1. What are the full details of the recommended operation?
2. Will you remove any lymph nodes? How many?
3. Will you take tissue samples?
4. Do you believe you will manage to 'debulk'? (i.e. remove all visible cancer)
5. Can you provide an overview of the operation?
6. How long can I expect to be in hospital?
7. What pain management will be planned?
8. What is my recovery time once home?
9. Will I need additional support once home?
10. What do you expect to achieve from this surgery?
11. How will surgery affect my prognosis?
12. How will surgery affect my quality of life?
13. How long will it take me to get back to normal after my surgery?
14. When can I take up my usual activities again?
15. In my position, would you have this surgery?
16. What are the risks involved in my surgery?
17. What are the implications if I decide not to have surgery?

18. Have you completed an operation this extensive previously?

19. Who will be involved in the operation? (i.e. who does the team consist of?)

20. Would I need specialist treatment in hospital such as intensive care following the surgery?

Questions Specific to My Surgery and Diagnosis

1. What you remove my omentum?
2. Will you remove part of my peritoneum?
3. Will you remove part of my bowel?
4. If I have surgery to remove part of my bowel would I require an ileostomy or a colostomy bag? How would this affect my quality of life?
5. Food is very important to me. Would a colostomy affect what I ate?
6. Would the colostomy be reversible at a later date?
7. At the time of my diagnosis I was informed I may be inoperable due to cancerous fluid in my lung, is this no longer a concern?
8. I know I require a complete surgical hysterectomy. Will I have more menopausal symptoms after my surgery?
9. Would I be able to take HRT?
10. How can I deal with menopausal symptoms if I don't take HRT?

Making the Time Count

The week before my surgery was also the week of my 31st birthday. My husband took some holiday from work and I made a list of things I wanted to do. I never said it to him at the time but death was with us at every moment. I was overwhelmed by the thought of not waking up from my surgery.

So, I had one week and I wanted to make it count. And, as a result, for the first time, I mindfully chose how to spend my time. I wasn't wasting a second. Nothing was taken for granted.

I told people how much they meant to me. I loved them without reservation. I had a picnic in a local park and invited everyone I knew (it was awesome). I went out for amazing meals - I'm a foodie after all. I went to an aquarium - I LOVE water – and declared to my husband that one day I would swim with the sharks in the tank. Do you know what? Seven months later I did just that! I spent time with my family. I spent lots of time with my dog and together we ran about in nature and I went to the theatre on dates with my hubby.

In those few days I learnt more about life and where my joy lies than I could have in a lifetime.

This is why I'm so grateful for my cancer. This is why I'm so positive and filled with love and joy and a childlike passion for life. And, if I'm totally honest, this is why I'm not ashamed to say that I love mermaids and unicorns and glitter; because cancer has enabled me to accept my authentic self.

The day before my surgery I planned to write letters to those who mattered most to me, just in case. In the end, I never did because I'm a strong believer of 'tempting fate' and fortunately those letters weren't needed as I'm still here. But, this gave me a hidden gift because now I know whom I would write a letter to if I had to say goodbye. I know every single soul in this world who means so much to me that I'd want to tell them. But that's not the gift. The real gift is I get to appreciate this knowledge every single day and make sure I show them so that, if the time comes, they won't need a letter.

Prehabilitation

Preparation for surgery is much more than just packing the right things and meeting all of your medical team. There is extensive research that shows that the fitter you are before surgery, the better chance you have of recovery afterwards. With that in mind, I spent every day in the lead up to my surgery ensuring that I went for a three mile walk with my dog. This not only helped to keep my body healthy but also my mind too. There was something wonderful about the time alone with my dog in the countryside.

On our last walk before my operation I took a photo and saved it as the screensaver on my tablet. I looked at it every day I was in hospital, promising myself I would go back to that spot. When I finally made it back there I felt elation at keeping my promise to myself.

After my older dog passed away in December 2016 I placed his ashes in the same spot. I still walk past there every day with my new dog, Ozzy, to remind myself just how far I have come both emotionally and physically. It a little daily reminder of just how precious life is.

Admission

In the days before my surgery I received multiple phone calls from the two hospitals involved in my care to let me know that my platelets were low and that, as a result, I would need to go into hospital two days early to have a blood transfusion before my surgery. I was absolutely devastated. I had big plans for spending the Saturday celebrating my 31st Birthday with my entire family before coming to the hospital on the Sunday but this news meant I'd be spending the time in a hospital ward which, let's be honest, is hardly the same.

We chatted about the possibility of me having a transfusion in my local hospital as a day patient so that I could have the Saturday at home but it just wasn't to be. So, instead, I spent my time running around my house getting ready for my admission in one evening, rather than over a few days as I'd originally planned. Cancer was once again reminding me that plans can change at any moment.

This involved, packing, cleaning and driving two hours to the hospital. We had rented a flat, through a friend of a friend, near to the hospital for my husband to use while I was recovering, so at least we were able to stay there for the night.

However, as it transpired, when the hospital took my blood tests that morning things weren't as they expected. My platelets were back to normal so I didn't need a transfusion after all. My white blood cells were low though, so I had to have an injection in my tummy to stimulate my bone marrow.

The trip wasn't wasted though. I got to meet my surgeon again and I also got to see the High Dependency Ward that I'd wake up in post surgery. This was very reassuring as it meant that I got to meet the nurses who would be caring for me and also got a sense of all the machinery I'd potentially be hooked up to. My imagination (as usual) had been much worse than reality. The nurses were wonderful and the ward wasn't nearly as terrifying as I'd thought. It was just like any other ward but with a few extra machines.

I can't begin to describe how happy I was to get out of the hospital and come home. After thinking I wasn't going to see my home for a few weeks it was amazing just how satisfying walking through our front door was. A bath had never felt so good, our bed had never been so comfortable and a home cooked meal had never tasted so good. As for seeing my pets again; it was utter heaven. Yes, I'd only been away for one night but I'd thought I'd be away for at least a month and I was so grateful to get more time before my surgery and subsequent recovery.

It never ceases to amaze me how often we can take these simple delights for granted. What a blessing it was to be reminded how lovely and fulfilling my life is and how many simple pleasures there are every day. Walks with my dog, my garden, time with family, a home cooked meal, cuddles on the sofa with my husband and cats, listening to music in the bath and sleeping in my own bed are all simple yet wonderful gifts for which I am now grateful for each and every day I am alive to enjoy them.

The Support of Others

My hubby and I, joined by my mum and dad, returned to the hospital the following week for my surgery. My blood results were showing that my platelets and white bloods cells were all at the right levels for surgery and I was given the all clear to go ahead. The night before, I was given the opportunity to meet my anaesthetist. This was really reassuring and I hope that it is an option available to all people facing surgery. We sat for some time going over the medication he would be using and the extra monitors he would be putting in place to ensure that my body wasn't under any unnecessary anxiety or stress during the surgery. He also explained that he would give me an epidural before surgery and leave it in for three days afterwards to help ensure that I had minimal distress and pain as I started my recovery. He explained everything really carefully to me and reassured me that I was in safe hands. I hadn't realised the level of my anxiety until after this meeting as I felt an emotional weight lifting from my shoulders.

That night I wanted to spend some time alone. I had begun to feel overwhelmed with all of the meetings and tests and I just needed some time to myself to process everything. My family were, fortunately, really understanding of this although I am sure they were desperate to spend every last minute with me.

It is really important in situations like this to do what feels right for you, not what is right for anyone else. You are the person facing the surgery and it is very individual how you might react. My advice is just to go with what feels best for you and your needs.

That night I felt the calmest I'd felt since I'd heard what my operation would involve. This was down to the medical team at the hospital I was in and the lovely messages I was receiving from my friends and family. It was also, without doubt, due to the messages I received from women around the world who'd had similar operations to what I had planned. Those messages came from women whom I'd never met, each discussing their treatment, operation and recovery in a way that comforted and reassured me that I was not alone. To this day I am so incredibly grateful to each and every one of them for being part of my journey. I now hope that by sharing my experience I offer the same reassurances to other women too.

The Big Day

I went down to theatre at 9.30am on Monday 9th May 2016, where I was taken straight in to have my epidural. Due to the requirement for me to be put to sleep immediately afterwards, my husband was unable to join me for this part and so, remembering what had happened the last time I'd had a general anaesthetic, I had been freaking out about it all morning but the anaesthetic team were exceptional. Recognising I was anxious they took their time talking to me and reassuring me. As it turns out my anaesthetist and I had a shared favourite Indian restaurant in my hometown so I was comforted as I talked to him about the food there as he did his work. As I mentioned previously, I am a self-declared foodie and, as a result, I'm easily distracted by the talk of Indian food.

Following the epidural, the team lay me down and got

me ready to be put to sleep. I thought I'd still be anxious at this point but they were very kind and kept talking to me until I drifted off. They also assured me that when my family saw me after surgery they would ensure that my head cap was back in place so they wouldn't see me without hair. This was a huge comfort to me as, although my family had all seen my bald head, it demonstrated that this team were caring about me as a whole person and were not just seeing me as a patient.

I don't remember much of being in the recovery room following surgery but I'm told I was in there for several hours. All I do really remember is a lot of people around my bed, beeping machines and falling in and out of consciousness. I also remember asking the anaesthetist if I had a colostomy bag. His gentle 'yes' filled my ears as I drifted back to sleep.

I also don't remember being taken to the High Dependency Unit (HDU) but I do remember my husband coming into my room. Mostly I remember his face, a mixture of relief and exhaustion. I know my parents and sisters came in to see me shortly afterwards too although I'm told it wasn't until about 1am by the time any of them were allowed in due to the length of the operation and the time it took to wake me. My sisters tell me that when they came into my room I proudly declared 'look at my scar' as I tried to move my covers out of the way. It is amazing (and amusing) what anaesthetic and painkillers will do to you.

The Aftermath

When I woke the next day I was in a whole new world. I slipped into sleep quickly and easily and I wasn't ever really aware of the time. Instead the passing of my days were marked by the many different medical and surgical staff coming to see me. At some point my surgeon came in to explain what had happened during surgery. My operation had lasted eleven hours during which they had conducted a complete hysterectomy - removing my cervix, womb, ovaries and right fallopian tube (I only had one prior to surgery due to my aforementioned ectopic pregnancy in August 2015). They had removed my omentum, my appendix, my spleen, part of my colon (resulting in a colostomy bag), part of my liver, part of my diaphragm, part of my pancreas and several abdominal lymph glands. None of this mattered though because, most importantly, they had successfully removed all visible signs of cancer.

This was certainly no small achievement with a stage four B cancer patient!

And, although I was still only part way through my journey, with two more chemotherapy doses still to receive and thirteen more monthly doses of Avastin, once I had recovered enough from surgery, it was exceptional news to hear.

I spent the rest of the week in HDU receiving oxygen and extensive pain relief. Although I tried to remember everything, after being told that people often forget their time in HDU, I remember only snippets. I had, however, asked my husband to take a daily photograph. This is something that he kindly obliged to do. Even now it frightens me to look at how ill I looked at that stage, but it also allows me to see the progress I have made since. For this reason I, perhaps controversially, recommend photos throughout your journey with adversity because one day you will look back on them and realise what an incredible warrior you really are.

My epidural was left in for a few days, however it only worked on my right hand side. As a result I struggled to move and I felt nauseated all of the time. In order for the nurses to check where the epidural was working they would rub a piece of ice over different parts of my abdomen and legs every couple of hours. This was an oddly settling sensation when you are lying in bed for days burning with heat. However, had the epidural been working properly, I wouldn't have felt the cold relief of the ice nor the pain that coursed through my body. I was in agony.

Having the epidural in for the first few days meant that I was unable to get out of bed and so the nurses had to change my bed with me still in it. This was a tricky task involving plastic pull sheets and a lot of discomfort. To this day I have no idea why they couldn't have just left the bed sheets, after all I was only in them for a few days and the pain and distress this caused each morning seemed inhumane.

The feeling of constant pain is hard to describe. It's never easy to get someone to understand what someone else is feeling, but I think the main factor with the pain was the frustration it caused me. I was suddenly unable to do so many things I'd taken for granted previously. I couldn't sit up or roll over without experiencing torturous agony. I couldn't wash myself or brush my teeth. I couldn't eat or drink due to the need for my colon to recover post surgery. The list went on and, at that stage, seemed endless. The light at the end of the tunnel was very dim.

A turning point for me was, three days following my operation, when two physiotherapists managed to help me to do a 60m walk using them and my drip for balance. Although I was completely exhausted the following day as a result, I began to realise that I was slowly overcoming all of the things I couldn't do and starting to build up the list of things I could. Taking advice from a friend who has had to overcome many physical challenges of her own, I started to make a mental note every time I achieved something I hadn't before: the first time I brushed my teeth unaided in bed; my first mouthful of food; the first time I managed to wipe my own face; the first time I managed to sit beside my bed rather than in it. Individually each of these were just baby steps yes, but collectively they were hugely significant in my journey to recovery.

One of the things I thought I would find most challenging was the nurses helping to wash me while I was still in bed. I thought it would be awful and degrading but, in reality, it was always done in a manner that ensured my utmost modesty and comfort. And, let's be honest, when you are in that much need of care and support you are beyond caring about such trivial things as how you are washed, so long as you are comfortable. That said, the first day I was able to wash my own face and arms while they just washed my legs and back was utter heaven.

Three days after surgery I was moved to a side room on a gynaecology ward. While this was a huge step in my recovery, I still continued to struggle with new daily physical and emotional battles. I felt nauseated all of the time and so didn't eat much which, as anyone who knows me will confirm, is completely out of character and so was hugely frustrating for me. I was unrecognisably thin and, as a result, I was completely exhausted all the time. I would fall asleep often and would struggle to converse due to breathlessness caused by the surgery on my diaphragm. I was in constant pain. While I was certainly not in the pain you would expect from such extensive surgery, thanks to so many drugs, I was obviously still sore. This upset me emotionally, rather than physically. Overnight I'd gone from walking every day to struggling to get out of bed unaided. I didn't know who I was anymore.

Emotional Pain

For a long time I struggled to come to terms with the extent of my surgery. Every time I thought about it I would feel physically sick. In particular, I felt a lot of anger and frustration all the time. As a result I would frequently break down, hysterical from the emotional and physical burdens surgery had left me with. One night I had to be sedated just so I could settle for a couple of hours while my incredible husband sat by my side until the early hours of the morning, holding my hand silently in the darkness.

No one prepared me for how hard it would be to emotionally recover from this part of my journey. You would anticipate such major surgery to be a physical battle but I think the emotional struggle played a much more significant role in inhibiting my recovery. Many aspects of my life had changed as a result of my operation and I feared the length of time it would take to learn to live in my new world. As a result, while I quickly made progress with my physical abilities, my emotional health deteriorated at an alarming rate. I was in a very dark place and, in all honesty, I was ready to give up.

It is deeply challenging to go through something that your nearest and dearest will never be able to relate to. I felt so alone and terrified all of the time. Even the medical staff didn't know how I felt. At this time I found myself grateful again for fellow warriors holding my hand on my journey, through their incredible support during this stage, and since, many great friendships have emerged.

I am a very positive person and I was completely caught off guard by how hard this part of the journey was. I would try my hardest to remind myself how far I'd come. Each day I knew I was physically improving but it didn't make an ounce of difference to my emotional recovery. Emotionally I was broken.

I felt caged and isolated; separated from a world I was no longer familiar with. I would watch as everyone's lives continued while mine stood still. I struggled with tasks that just weeks before I had taken for granted. I no longer knew the body I found myself in. For the first time in my journey I saw a cancer patient looking at me from inside the mirror. Her eyes were sunken, her skin grey. She had fluffy, dark tufts of hair. Her bones stuck out at all angles. Her legs were the size and shape of a child's because she had lost the muscle acquired from years of running. Her body was marked with too many scars to count. Her arms and legs black and blue from daily blood tests, injections and cannula sites. Her eyes had lost their sparkle. Her face had lost its smile. She was a stranger. I didn't know her, nor did I want to. She was not welcome. She was sick. She was vulnerable. She was a cancer patient. She was no longer me.

Each day there were improvements of course. I had come miles physically. I knew this in my heart and I would try to reflect on it, but my spirit remained crushed. I constantly cried. I would sit and I would sob, not caring who saw or heard. I sobbed for the loss of the life I had. I sobbed for the life the people closest to me had lost, knowing all too well how deeply my suffering affected them. I sobbed for others on their own cancer journey; both for those I knew and those I didn't.

One of the hardest parts for me was the needles. I didn't have an issue with needles before, in fact I was a blood donor for many years. Post surgery, however, it was a very different story. My already delicate veins had been shrunken by chemotherapy. A venflon (the needle attached to an IV drip) should last four days but in me it was lasting just one before the site would swell and it would need to be removed. Replacing it would take several attempts, usually involving more than one person. As a result I would require up to five needles going into my arms and hands each day just for my drip, on top of this I would require twice-daily blood tests. Again these would take several attempts each time. I also required daily anti-blood clotting injections into my thighs each night. Finally, I had to have a number of vaccinations due to my splenectomy. Adding this up, I calculated that in the weeks following surgery I had over 250 needles pierce my skin.

As a result, my veins were swollen and raw and my skin was varying shades of blues, purples and greens. I found the sight of a member of my medical team coming towards me with their white tray of needles unbearable. At one point I broke down on the third attempt for a blood sample from my hands. I had tried for so long to remain strong but the emotional strain was now reflecting in physical pain. I was a shadow of my former positive self and I felt I would never grasp that reality again.

I remember turning to my husband and telling him that I understood why people gave up. The thought of going on and continuing with this suffering felt unbearable. That day my sister came to visit me with her four children. As she placed her eight-week-old baby in my arms I realised I couldn't give up. How could I cause these innocent souls any unnecessary suffering? From that moment I made a conscious decision to do everything in my power to heal myself, to regain my strength and return to whole. They were too young to understand at the time but I owe my life to those four beautiful souls. Through their love I reminded myself that I would get there. I reminded myself how far I had come. I began to realise that this was just another mountain to climb and that the view at the top would be more than worth it. I knew my journey was long. I knew my journey was challenging. Most importantly, though, I knew that with the love and support of others, my journey was possible.

In the meantime I was brave and strong and broken but I was a warrior and I knew I would survive.

Some Light at the End of the Tunnel

Slowly each day, bit by bit, my spirit lifted. The medical team understood how fiercely independent I was before my operation and supported me to rebuild my strength and confidence with little trips outside. At one point my surgeon even let my hubby and I escape for an hour to visit the seaside. It was magical. My soul was overjoyed and I finally caught a glimpse of my old self.

Within days I was allowed to return home. It was just sixteen days following my major operation and, although I was still highly medicated, I was deemed well enough to make the two-hour car journey home. I was overjoyed but I was also terrified.

In hospital, despite my constant pain and emotional decline, I had felt safe. In hospital I knew that there would always be someone on hand to support me if anything went wrong. Hospital had become my security blanket and overnight I was forced to return to a painful reality.

I had completely underestimated the pain the two hour journey from the hospital would cause my body. I'd also completely underestimated how little I would be able to do and how much I would have to rely on my husband. Suddenly, over night, he had to take on the role of an entire medical team, including administering nearly 30 tablets a day, while simultaneously looking after our house and our 'zoo' of pets. He really was (and continues to be) my superhero.

A few hours into my first day I was once again lying on the floor screaming in pain. I was emotionally and physically in pieces and I felt completely out of my depth. In too much pain to move, I was unable to take the breakthrough morphine I'd been provided for this very situation and instead lay surrounded by cushions on our kitchen floor until I found the strength. Again I faced the painful choice - the choice of quit of continue. This one felt harder than while I'd been in hospital. I saw the pain in my husband's eyes and knew I was the cause. I also knew there would be more days like this, that there would be more pain to come. But I saw something else in his eyes too. I saw love. With his support I made it through to our living room and onto the sofa where I finally took some morphine tablets and instantly I fell asleep.

The following two days showed gradual improvement. Although I would wake up several times through the night in pain, I was now taking the breakthrough morphine as soon as I needed it. I was still sometimes being sick but I was also managing to eat small mouthfuls and with the support of district nurses and my GP making regular home visits, the light at the end of the tunnel began to shine a little brighter.

During this time I learnt an invaluable lesson about the power of the mind. Months prior to my surgery I had bought front row tickets to see one of my favourite comedians in a local venue (Nina Conti in case you are wondering). The date of the show, however, was just over two weeks following my operation. In a bid to pick me up my Macmillan nurse contacted the venue to explain my health condition and arranged for me to meet Nina back stage if I made it to the show. It was a big 'if'. Talk about having a goal. There was no way on Earth I was going to miss the opportunity.

So I willed myself well and by some miracle, I made it to the show and indeed met her afterwards. Looking at the photos of our meeting you could never even tell I was unwell let alone that I had just come out of a high dependency ward following major surgery. Little did I know at the time something major and life threatening was silently taking hold of my body.

Darkness Descends

After an amazing evening meeting Nina Conti, things turned bad, really bad.

When we returned home after the show, I went to bed feeling only a little more sore and tired than the previous few days but nothing to really complain about. Then through the night I was up three times to take breakthrough morphine to help with the pain. I had, of course, expected to feel pain after braving a trip to the theatre so soon after my discharge from hospital but this was crazy pain. I was in agony.

Morning soon arrived and with it a whole new set of issues. I couldn't stop being sick. Every time I tried to eat anything I was sick. This was an issue. I needed to eat to take my tablets and my tablets were my pain relief - so now I had uncontrollable sickness and pain. I spent most of that day in bed, except for when the district nurse came round for her daily visit to change one of my dressings. She offered to call in a doctor but I thought I had things under control and declined, returning to bed for more rest. As evening came my symptoms began to settle as I finally managed to keep my tablets down. I thought I'd overcome the worst of my symptoms and went to bed hopeful of better things the next day.

How wrong was I.

During the night I woke to a pain I didn't think was humanly possible to feel. I remember vividly thinking death would surely be a more humane option than the suffering I was feeling. Medication wouldn't stay down and even a sip of water resulted in continuous vomiting. It was time to admit defeat. Something was seriously wrong. This wasn't just a case of overdoing it by going to the theatre. Death had, once again, entered the room.

My husband called the national cancer helpline for advice. For the first time ever no one answered. He was panicked and I was now on a different planet with the pain. Now unable to move and hardly able to speak I remember mumbling for him to call 999. He did and was told it wasn't an issue for them and that they would get NHS 24 to call him back.

He tried the cancer helpline again and, thankfully, this time someone answered straight away. After he explained the situation they transferred him to the oncology ward at the hospital where I was receiving treatment and they agreed I needed to be admitted and that they would send an ambulance.

I don't remember much after that but I think I kept falling in and out of sleep. I do remember that every time I came to my husband was sitting by my side ensuring I was okay. He has told me since that it was two hours before the ambulance arrived.

When the paramedics did arrive they came upstairs to our bedroom and strapped me to a seated stretcher so that they could carry me downstairs and across our driveway to the ambulance. It was early daylight by this point and I remember a misty rain hitting my skin. I was shaking from anxiety and pain and wrapped tight in a blanket but the rain on my face was refreshingly comforting nonetheless. Little did I know it would be weeks before I would return home again.

The paramedics soon had me strapped onto the trolley in the ambulance and one of them held me during the drive. I remember him reassuring me the whole journey to the hospital, telling me we would be there soon and that my husband would meet us there. I didn't know at the time that the ambulance was flashing its emergency blue lights as we sped our way to hospital.

By the time we arrived I was a mix of exhaustion and anxiety but I so vividly recall one of the oncology nurses, who had treated me when I had been diagnosed just months previously, taking my hand as I arrived and saying 'hello stranger' as she smiled warmly at me. The tension leaving my body as a result of this simple, yet warm, gesture was palpable. I knew I could relax.

On the ward there was already a doctor waiting to put a cannula into my arm so that an IV of fluids and pain relief could be connected. Obviously by this stage I was dehydrated to say the least. Bloods were taken too and my surgery site was checked over before I was sent for chest and abdominal x-rays.

I'm not sure when my husband arrived. In my memory he was there the whole time but I know that's not possible because he had to sort out our pets and gather together my medication and bags before even following the ambulance. I do remember, once the IV fluids started to take effect and the lovely hospital morphine was masking the pain, that the nurses sat with us and comforted us. They gave us so much support. They made us laugh. They reassured us. They were everything and more and I am so eternally grateful. I remember one saying to my husband that they appreciated what he must have gone through in the last thirty-six hours and that he was to go home and sleep because I was safe now. I loved the fact that they weren't just treating me but instead seeing us as a whole unit entwined in this cancer journey. I think people can underestimate how much cancer affects those closest to the person with cancer too, and not just the person with cancer themselves. The people in my life who ask me how Ewan is doing, rather than just checking in on me, have become my favourite people.

Finding the Root of the Problem

The following morning I was taken for a CT scan. I

hate CT scans. However, it was of course painless and fine. The staff were wonderful and it was over in less than five minutes. More importantly, while the X-rays had been clear, the CT scan started to give some indication of what was causing my pain and sickness.

It appeared that there was a 'collection' sitting behind my liver. A 'collection' of what remained the question - Blood? Fluid? Cancer? Infection?

The infection markers from my blood tests indicated the latter and so I was soon prescribed a range of strong antibiotics to be administered continuously via IV. I was still getting fluids and also had a syringe driver administering constant morphine and anti-sickness. Things felt under control and, although I was upset to be back in hospital, I began to accept that it was the place where I needed to be.

A week later, however, and I was still in hospital. After my emergency admission the following few days had been spent trying to get my symptoms under control. I continued to get antibiotics and fluids continuously, alongside morphine and anti-sickness medication. I'd also had three blood transfusions to help stabilise my blood results. Sickness continued to be an issue and I could no longer eat anything. Just one or two mouthfuls and I was still being sick. I asked to be weighed and was horrified to discover I'd lost a further ten kilos in two weeks. During this time in hospital I went down to a weight of just forty-two kilos. I was unrecognisable.

I remember when I got diagnosed someone said to me 'you just need to eat, drink and go to the toilet. Let the medical team take care of everything else.' I didn't understand what she'd meant at the time, but I did when my weight started to plummet at an unhealthy rate. I couldn't control the drugs or medical interventions. The doctors couldn't control my eating and drinking. Together we could work towards me recovering from this trauma.

In order to treat my condition I had to see an intervention radiologist in theatre to have my infection drained. I was scheduled to be sedated for the procedure, however, due to a miscommunication with the ward staff, I ate breakfast on the day of the procedure and, as a result, I was unable to receive the sedative. Once again, I found myself unnecessarily awake for a painful procedure and experiencing pain and distress that I could have been spared. However, always one to look on the bright side, this meant that I got to watch the whole process and it was fascinating. The radiologist used an ultrasound and x-ray machine to locate the abscess that had shown on my earlier CT scan. Once it had been located he injected local anaesthetic into the area while a nurse started to administer pain relief through an IV. The radiologist then began cutting through the layers on my abdomen and, initially, all I could feel was pressure. Suddenly, however, I was hit with stabbing pain and, I am not ashamed to admit, I screamed. He reassured me and injected more local anaesthetic while I was simultaneously given more IV pain relief. Once I was comfortable enough to proceed he went ahead with the final cut. It was excruciating! I burst into tears. He again reassured me and explained that he had been unable to numb the abscess wall and that's why I had experienced pain.

His next step was to insert a tube into the abscess and

drain some samples for the lab. Following this a drain bag was attached and the tube was stitched and tapped in place. I was then lifted back onto my hospital bed and changed into a new gown as mine was now stained with blood. The team were exceptional. They explained everything, comforted me and even had music playing during the procedure. It really was an educational experience.

What drained from the abscess over the next couple of days was disgusting. The bag that had been stitched in place slowly filled with a thick, brown, lumpy liquid that you definitely wouldn't want hanging about in your body, least of all around your liver.

Although I'd been told it could be up to five days before the lab would be able to determine if what was being drained was an infection, just a few hours following the procedure the ward received a phone call to say that the lab were already growing things from the samples. This confirmed that I had a form of sepsis.

At the time, despite the constant monitoring and extensive treatment, I didn't realise how serious my condition was. I later discovered that the sepsis - a blood infection – had built up on my liver as a result of my surgery. This is serious and dangerous for anyone but for someone, like me, who had recently had their spleen removed and, as a result, had an impaired immune system, it is life threatening. In fact, I have since discovered that at this stage in my journey I had less than a 30% chance of survival. I was literally knocking on death's door.

The Road to Health

I cannot stress enough how person-centred my medical team were. At the time of hearing I had sepsis on my liver I had been in hospital for nearly a month with the exception of the three days I'd spent at home prior to my emergency admission. I was emotionally in a dark place and physically weaker than I'd ever been. Recognising this my team worked together to make things as comfortable as possible for me. Within an hour of my confirmed diagnosis they had made the decision that I didn't need to receive fluids anymore as my blood tests showed that my levels were stable. They also switched all but one of my antibiotics to oral tablets. This meant that I instantly went from being attached to an IV drip 24/7 to needing it only three hours twice daily. As a result, for the first time in over a week, I was able to have some time during the day when I wasn't attached to a drip. After so long this felt like a massive step in the right direction. More importantly, this meant that I was now free to leave the hospital between lunch and dinner as long as my husband was with me.

Within moments I went from a hopeless lost soul to taking a huge step towards my old self. That afternoon my husband brought my dog Robbie to visit me outside the hospital. I'm not sure who was more pleased to see one another. With me sitting in a wheelchair we slowly explored the woodlands on the hospital grounds. It was magical. I felt so free. I was me again, walking my dog with the man I love. I still had my syringe driver and drain attached, I was still weak, I was still in pain, but I was happy and really, when it comes down to it, what more can we really ask for from life?

The following day (Sunday) my husband took me to the local Botanic Gardens in a wheelchair. The buzz I got from being in nature again was just indescribable. The grass had never been greener, the flowers had never been more fragrant, the sky had never been bluer. Slowly my soul was healing.

On the Monday I was visited by my consultant; a wonderful woman, who treats me rather than my diagnosis. She agreed that I would heal faster at home and that our focus needed to be to get me detached from all the medical equipment. First step was to speak to the lab about the samples of sepsis taken from my body to discover what oral antibiotics would best treat it. Their response enabled me to be switched to just one antibiotic - rather than four. I was disconnected from the drip completely and the painful venflon was finally removed from my arm.

On the Tuesday I was sent for an ultrasound scan to see if my drain could be removed. This would be dependent on all of the infection having successfully drained. I was so anxious for good news, knowing that this would determine how much longer I needed to remain in hospital.

Following this the staff made the decision to remove the drain. They also made the decision to remove my syringe driver and try me back on oral pain relief and to stop my anti sickness medication. It was a lot of fast changes in a very short space of time but it was all positive. I was making progress. I was moving onwards in my journey and, more importantly, I was moving in the right direction.

Suddenly I was free from attachments. I felt able to straighten my aching body again. I was able to move more freely. I'd regained a sense of self. That day when I showered I wasn't coordinating my usual juggling act of medical equipment. It was just me, standing under the healing water. Oh what bliss. The little things in life we take for granted really are all that matter in the bigger picture. They are wherein lies the joy. That day, for the first time since I'd been admitted two weeks before, I got dressed following my shower. No longer did I want to sit in my pyjamas. I was feeling better and I was getting to go home.

The cancer patient I had faced in the mirror was fading, my sense of self was returning and the light at the end of the tunnel was shining bright. I had made it through another phase in my journey. It was tough. I'd seen darkness, I'd felt pain, I'd faced my greatest fears, but I hadn't let it break me. I felt stronger for knowing the experiences I had faced and survived. I felt better for the people I had met who had cared for me. Above all I felt inspired and encouraged by the healing power I'd found within and the love and care in the world.

I had become a warrior.

Top Tips - What to Pack for Hospital

While everyone will have a different list of priority items to pack, here is my top ten 'must haves' for a long hospital stay.

1. Earplugs and an Eye Mask: Sleep is one of the

most important things for healing yet, ironically, one of the hardest things to do on a hospital ward. It's noisy and you have no control over when it's 'lights out' (unless you are lucky enough to have a side room). Earplugs and an eye mask are lifesavers in this situation.

2. Nice Toiletries: Let's be honest you are in hospital for a reason so you are probably going to be feeling pretty crap. Some nice toiletries can make all the difference. If you will be able to have a shower while in hospital then take a nice shower gel. One that smells amazing. Moisturisers are essential too as your skin will get very dry and you'll always feel better after using some cream, especially on your face. Personally I just use coconut oil. Wet wipes are also a must have! They allow you to quickly freshen up and feel more human when you get some visitors, even if you are unable to have a proper wash. I love essential oils and so always take a few of my favourites if I am going into hospital. Not only can they help with your emotional health but they smell amazing too. Lavender and geranium are great for helping you to rest and frankincense is a personal favourite of mine too.

3. An Extra Long Charging Cable: You'll usually find a plug high up on the wall behind your hospital bed that you can use to plug in and charge your electronic devices. However, if you are charging with just a normal length cable then you will be unable to use the device or have to contort your body to do so because the cable won't reach your bed. An extra long cable (I use a 3m one) helps resolve this and means you can always be connected to the outside world.

4. An Electronic Tablet: In the weeks following

recovery from my surgery my tablet was a lifesaver. I was able to watch films, listen to music, stay in touch with people through social media and, of course, update my blog! Most evenings my hubby would sit in the chair beside my hospital bed while we caught up on our favourite TV dramas on my tablet too. This allowed some normality into our lives and was as close to cuddling on our sofa as we would get while I was in hospital.

Another electronic device I took was my phone and, of course, headphones are essential too.

5. A V-Shaped Pillow: These large pillows are amazing after major surgery. They are super comfy and 'hug' your body as you lean on them, meaning that you feel fully supported. Not only did I use mine every day in hospital but also in the months following and whenever I went for chemo. In fact, I still use it now. These are available in most homeware shops and are inexpensive.

6. Bed Wear: I love pyjamas and any excuse to buy new ones. Always make sure you take plenty of pairs with you into hospital. These are your clothes and bed wear while you're in so you'll be wanting them washed (by a helpful loved one) on a regular basis. Having lots of pairs with you ensures you have enough to keep you going.

Take a nice cotton (not fluffy!) dressing gown too. It allows you to keep yourself decent when your in-laws or colleagues (for example) visit without becoming roasting hot or feeling like you are obviously in your pyjamas.
Comfortable slippers with a rubber sole help for when moving around the ward without the risk of slipping.
7. Two Drawstring Bags for Laundry: The helpful

loved one doing your washing doesn't really want to have to touch it. By packing two cotton drawstring bags you can fill one with your dirty washing. Then, once full, it can be taken away and popped in a washing machine with your dirty clothes still inside. Your lovely, helpful loved one can then handle and dry the clothes and bag once they are nice and clean and out of the machine. In the meantime you can start filling the other bag to repeat the process.

8. Sensible Pants: In my experience of being in hospital, other people (doctors, nurses etc.) see you in your underwear a lot! For instance previously when I was in for a hip operation I had doctors needing to draw on my hip before surgery, check the site after surgery and nurses injecting anti-blood clot medication into my thigh each day. While I'm sure the staff don't care what your underwear looks like, you'll certainly feel much less self-conscious if you have some 'sensible pants' on rather than your best French lace when they are checking you over. Time to buy some super sized undies!

9. Colouring Books/Puzzles/Games/Books: I recommend taking a range of different activities. Sometimes you will be up for reading and sometimes your brain won't manage it due to medication, pain or tiredness. Also remember when planning what activities you will likely want to do while in hospital that your brain will be in a very different state from normal.

10. Games for Visitors: When you're in hospital you spend a lot of your time with visitors and sometimes you want to talk about your health and sometimes you don't. A good distraction is to have a couple of games on hand (or ask them to bring one). My personal favourites are travel battleships, travel 4x4 and 'Cards Against Humanity'. The latter is definitely not one to play with Grandma, although my Mum and Dad are both huge fans!

Top Tips - Ideas for What to Take When Visiting Someone in Hospital

If you are visiting someone in hospital following major surgery it can be hard to know what to take with you. First of all, trust me when I say they will just be happy to see you and won't care if you come empty handed but if you are still keen here are the things I found most helpful:

1. Magazines: I'm not into 'gossip magazines' at all but what I do like magazines about nice homes and homeware. These are easy to read and take very little brainpower. This is perfect when you are feeling highly medicated. I still remember fondly, when one of my sisters brought bridal magazines into the hospital so we could start planning her wedding!

2. Healthy Snacks: Hospital food is usually awful – well it is in my experience anyway. Also, as meals come at set times you can often be left hungry in between meals. I would wake up in the middle of the night starving with nothing available to eat. Friends and family started bringing in healthy snacks that could be stored out of the fridge, such as nuts and dried fruit. This was great as it meant I always had food to hand right by my bed.

3. Fruit Juice or Smoothies: This is a personal

favourite for me. Following major surgery it can be hard to eat big meals and therefore weight loss, and sometimes malnutrition, becomes inevitable. Fruit juice and smoothies are a great way to get some vitamins back into your body. I had one friend even bring a mini blender into the hospital so that I could make my own. This may sound crazy but, in reality, I think this played a major part in my recovery. Even just taking in a carton of fresh orange juice can make a huge difference. I am salivating just remembering the joy it was to have a cold glass of juice after weeks in hospital.

4. Interesting Conversation: The person you are visiting in hospital most likely won't want to talk about hospital. Be sure to turn up with some funny stories to keep them interested. If nothing else it will make you both laugh which, incidentally, has been evidenced at helping the body to heal at a faster rate. Double win!

5. Photos and/or Cards: I was in hospital for weeks following my operation and one of my most precious things was the photos of my niece and nephews on the wall of my side room, as well as the cards and drawings I was sent. In the darkest hours of my recovery where I would be lying in bed, wide awake in the middle of the night, alone and stricken with grief one look at these gave me enough hope to get through to the next day, and the next. Never underestimate the power of something so simple as a heartfelt message in a card.

CHAPTER 5: LIFE AFTER TREATMENT

July-August 2016

The following few months, after finally returning home, were by no means uneventful. Chemotherapy post surgery was much harder than the treatment I had received previously as my already weakened body was still trying to recover from an extensive operation. As a result I had several unplanned hospital admissions during this time. Thankfully none involved as long a stay as previously but all brought the fear that I wouldn't make it home. My emotional health during this stage in my journey was still in need of repair.

When it came time for my final chemotherapy post surgery in July 2016 I thought I would be buzzing at the prospect of not having to go through the brutal side effects again. In reality, however, I found myself faced with mixed emotions.

On the one hand I was, of course, relieved. No more

hours of sitting connected to an IV. No more chemotherapy related hospital admissions. Instead my body would finally be able to start recovering from months of treatment - a process that, I was told, would take up to one year.

On the other hand, however, I felt afraid. The chemo had been 'attacking' my cancer for over six months. It had been doing its job to remove my cancer and I couldn't help but silently question 'What will happen when chemo stops?', 'Will what I've received be enough?, 'Will I hear the magical word 'remission' following my final scan?', 'What if I don't?', 'What if cancer still occupies my body?', 'What if I went through all of that for nothing?'

However, I soon realised that ending chemotherapy treatment would open me up to the next phase in my journey. At the time it was an unknown phase and, as a result, it's only natural (and healthy) to enter into it with questions.

Moments of Vulnerability

During this time I had deeply painful moments of feeling truly vulnerable, alone and helpless and it was terrifying. Out of nowhere anxiety would sneak up on me when I least expected it. I could be walking around a shop, for example, and suddenly I'd feel overwhelmingly alone and weak. Instantly I'd become scared. Scared I'd collapse. Scared I'd not make it around the shop. Scared someone would see me. Scared someone wouldn't.

I would walk around the shop slowly, leaning on my

trolley for strength and stability. People would pass, caught up in their lives. Their laughter and conversation would encircle me but I would feel separated from it as if submerged under water, watching from a distance. The world around me felt untouchable, like I was no longer part of it. I would feel completely disconnected from those around me.

The most frightening part was the feeling of being unseen. Feeling like, while I was disconnected from those around me, they too were disconnected from me. A feeling of helplessness, like if I were to collapse no one would stop, no one would see, no one would care. Of course, on reflection and with a level head I now know this to be untrue, but in those moment - those moments of fear and isolation - that is how I felt.

Upon reaching my car the effort of lifting my single bag of shopping proved to be unbearable. Again people passed, oblivious to the internal trauma I was facing as I battled physical and emotional fatigue. Getting into the car I would lock the doors, feeling safe behind a tangible barrier that physically, rather than emotionally, separated me from the world. Then I would sit and sob loud uncontrollable sobs.

The moments always passed. I would compose myself, regain emotional and physical strength and return home exhausted from the emotional ordeal.

I can't help but think of all the times I may have walked past someone going through a similar internal battle and not seen the person caught within the silent struggle. Perhaps if each of us were all to just take a moment in our days to see if someone may need a hand, a kind word, a smile, a nod, or just a little comradeship then maybe the world would feel a little safer and more welcoming to those in need. After all, we all feel vulnerable sometimes.

Remission

In August 2016, almost a year to the day following my surgery for an ectopic pregnancy, I heard the words I'd longed to hear 'you're in remission.' In the space of just eight months I had gone from having cancer throughout my abdominal and chest cavity to there being 'no evidence of disease'.

While I 'should' have been elated I instead felt deflated! While everyone around me was celebrating the news that my cancer had 'gone', I knew all to well that stage four B cancer is incurable and that, in medical terms 'remission' just means 'short break'. My oncologist explained clearly to me that my cancer would likely return and while I accepted this completely, I often felt that those around me did not.

Of course, before my own diagnosis, I too used to think that when someone was in remission that they were all better, that their cancer was gone and things could 'return to normal'. Now I know the frustration that this misconception can cause a cancer warrior. The end of chemotherapy (and even remission) can be a scary time for us warriors - perhaps even scarier than the cancer diagnosis itself. After months of support and treatment prescribed solely to treat our cancer, we can suddenly feel completely alone. Our 'medical' lifeline is now gone.

Don't get me wrong, I'd dreamt of my last day of chemotherapy for months. With each treatment I counted down the number of sessions left before I could say I was free from chemo. But, deep inside, it felt like my security blanket had been pulled away from me.

During this time, I came to realise that one of the hardest parts of living with stage four B cancer is people not appreciating what that actually means: that, in reality, you are living with cancer, essentially, for the rest of your life. Unlike some cancers, it is not 'curable' and, as such, it does not 'go away'. You do not 'get better'. You live your life in spite of it or, as I like to think, because of it. It can be so frustrating when people don't understand this or when they think that because my treatment had finished I must be 'all better'.

Living with cancer has highs and lows. I feel extremely blessed for every day I have and try my hardest to live my life as best I can. Some days that means piling on my makeup and going to a comedy show. Other days, however, it means pulling on my yoga trousers and meditating in the garden. Whatever each day brings I will not let cancer defeat my spirit. I will smile, I will look as well as I possibly can and I will laugh each and every day that I am blessed to be alive.

Life after treatment, and my subsequent transition to living with cancer, took a long time during which I had several unexpected admissions to hospital. There were many times during my recovery where I would feel sudden pain and before I knew it I was mentally and emotionally back in the dark place I'd been in previously. I became terrified of being admitted again and the prospect of something going seriously wrong.

On one such occasion I was admitted to hospital during the night. I vividly recall lying on the floor writhing in pain while a nurse tried desperately to place a cannula in my hand.

As I lay there unable to move from the pain and sickness I wondered 'does it ever go away? The fear? The illness? The anger? Is this the best it gets?'

Every ache, every pain, every twinge, every new sensation brought with it the lingering thought 'is this cancer?' No longer did I just get a headache. No it must be a brain tumour. The pain in my side couldn't be from overdoing it. No it must mean the cancer on my lungs had returned. Upset tummy? That's definitely the cancer spreading. No matter how positive I was in the day to day, the here and now, the fear was always just a moment away, waiting.

The following morning I woke in a world I had grown all too familiar with. There I was, once again, lying in a hospital bed. Suddenly I was overwhelmed with grief. I was grieving my admission to hospital; I was grieving my extensive treatment and diagnosis; I was grieving my loss of the life I'd had before cancer. However, despite these negative feelings about being in hospital, when I was told I could go home (having discovered that my admission had been caused by low magnesium which was easily fixable through supplements) I burst into tears. Soon I was gasping for breath, my legs gave way and my heart started to race. I felt like I couldn't breathe. My husband ran to get a nurse and when they took my pulse it was 157. I was put in a wheelchair and placed in a side room where a doctor immediately did a heart trace that, thankfully, was fine although my blood pressure was very low.

My issue, it appeared, wasn't physical. My issue was panic. Anxiety, that I had been pushing aside and refusing to acknowledge, was rearing its ugly head.

For weeks I'd been focusing so much on my physical health that I'd left my emotional health unchecked. I had stopped meditating. I had stopped spending time in nature. I had stopped treating my health holistically.

After some rest, and once my heart rate had returned to normal, I was allowed home. This time I felt calmer. I recognised what was happening and that I needed to make changes. When we got home my husband and I both fell asleep, joined by our beautiful rescue dog. When we woke, a few hours later, one of my sisters had visited and left a surprise gift. She'd secretly been collecting messages from friends in a notebook for me, waiting for the perfect moment to give it to me. This was certainly that moment. My face streamed with tears as I read my loved ones' words. It was the most beautiful gift I'd ever been given. It was the gift of love.

I knew then that I needed to make changes. I needed to pick myself up fast and that's exactly what I did. Over the next week I made several steps to start focusing on recovering my emotional and spiritual health and wellbeing.

As a result of these changes I felt transformed. I once again felt in touch with my sense of self, my values and my holistic approach to remaining healthy.

To this day I am so glad I had that panic attack because it demonstrated to me the importance of focusing on the three key aspects of my health - physical, emotional and spiritual - if I was to have any hope of returning to wholeness and awakening the healing power within.

Top Tips - How to Care for Your Emotional Health After Cancer

1. Write down all of your favourite activities. Do them. I wrote down beauty treatments, time in nature, going to the cinema, comedy shows, eating out, spending time with loved ones. I then made plans to include these in my life as much as possible. For example, I booked a beauty treatment for every week over the two months following the end of my treatment.

2. Seek help and support from professionals. I went to see my GP and spoke honestly about how I was feeling. I told her that I felt 'flat' and disengaged. I explained the loss of my normal routine since surgery, the frustration I felt from being too weak to walk our dog and my inability to drive while recovering from surgery. She listened, not rushing me so she could see her next patient, but instead supporting me to make a plan.

I also started seeing a psychologist. We only had a few sessions but they helped me tremendously. At the time of my diagnosis I was training to qualify as a hypnotherapist and psychotherapist and so I have a lot of respect for talking therapies. Despite this, I had never seen a therapist before but found I was able to talk very openly about my prognosis and treatment and also about other people's responses. She validated my emotions, explaining that how I was feeling was 'normal' and something she called 'good grief'. Sometimes, when you are feeling anxious, and also maybe a little scared, all you need to hear is that it's okay to feel what you are feeling.

3. Spend time in nature. I started walking my dog again. Just little five minute walks with my husband at first but slowly we built this up and just two weeks later we were enjoying thirty-minute walks most days. Today I walk at least an hour each day. This wouldn't have been possible without those first five minutes.

4. Share kindness with others. I started giving out random acts of kindness to strangers (more on this later). They gave me focus. They gave me purpose. Most of all, they gave me joy! The ripple effects continue to uplift me in ways that nothing else can.

5. Eat better. I started cooking more of the beautiful, healthy home made meals I had done prior to surgery, focusing on using fresh organic ingredients proven for their health promoting qualities.

6. Meditate. I started meditating again. Remaining mindful and focusing on the present moment, rather than letting the past or potential future influence your emotions is key to remaining positive and enjoying life. I'd lost touch with this in the weeks following surgery and, as a result, my positivity had wavered.

7. Read. Prior to my surgery I'd immersed myself in learning all I could about cancer and cancer treatment. However, since my surgery I had lost that focus and with it, I'd lost one if my greatest passions in life: new knowledge. I had also forgotten about the joy of reading a novel and losing yourself in another person's story.

Top Tips - How to Supporting Someone After Treatment

If you are not going through cancer treatment yourself, but instead find yourself caring for someone who has been diagnosed, there is so much you can do to support your loved one during their treatment. However, I want to draw attention to the invaluable support you can offer *after* treatment is completed because it is a phase in their journey that no one ever really wants to talk about.

This is my list of the 'dos and don'ts' for helping a loved one after treatment:

Do:

- Ask them how they are feeling about this stage in their journey.

- Ask what support they need - they may want to celebrate or they may want to cry.

- Understand that this can be one of the scariest times in a cancer journey and, also, the most likely time for support from their social network to cease - be the one to stand by them when everyone else walks away.

- If they chose to open up to you, listen. Really listen. They may want to talk about outcomes you don't want to hear about but they need to say those thoughts out loud so that they are no longer as frightening as they seem in their head or even, sometimes, just so they can laugh at how ridiculous they are being.

- Ask if they need you at any follow up appointments.

- Respect their decisions regarding their treatment, even (maybe especially) when you don't agree with them.

- Respect that they also may not want to talk about cancer anymore. They may wish to cease being labelled as 'your friend with cancer' and just return to being 'your friend'.

Don't:

- Presume that they feel the same way as you do about this stage in their journey.

- Compare them to other cancer warriors -

everyone is different, even those with the exact same diagnosis.

- Tell them everything will be okay. You don't know that and it can stop them from feeling that they can open up to you.

- Only talk to them about cancer. They are still interested in all the same things that they were prior to their diagnosis. They are still the same person.

PART THREE

DISCOVERING THE WARRIOR WITHIN

CHAPTER 6: RECURRENCE

December 2017

I had sixteen beautiful months where my cancer remained stable. This time was, of course, peppered with check ups, but, although my cancer markers were gently rising, my scans weren't showing any evidence of progression.

So, despite the fear of my cancer returning never truly being very far from my mind, when it finally did it caught me completely by surprise. I now know that no amount of fear or anxiety could have prepared me for that moment, a moment far worse than my initial diagnosis.

It was December 2017 and bitterly cold. For several days I'd had increasing pain in my right shoulder, ribs and the right hand side of my chest. I was uncomfortable, grumpy and anxious that something was wrong. However, everyone around me constantly reassured me that my scan just two months previously had been clear and so I gave myself a serious pep talk, reminding myself that if I'm still breathing then there is more right with me than wrong with me and I should keep focusing on what I *can* do rather than what I *can't*.

I reminded myself that all of our bodies are inherently healthy and that they want to survive, and that moping and worrying wasn't going to help my body to heal. Instead I knew that doing what gives me joy is the best thing for my body, mind and spirit. So before the sun had even risen to greet the new day, I pulled on my running shoes, covered my messy 'bed hair' with one of my old chemo head scarfs and went for a freezing cold run through our local woodlands as the sun rose over the surrounding hills. Little did I know that, this time, it wasn't just anxiety.

That night the stabbing pain in my chest was unrelenting. I am a self proclaimed hypochondriac, worsened by the fear of a cancer recurrence, and so I tried to ignore it as I sat on the sofa cuddled into my hubby's arms. However, my instinct was telling me that something was seriously wrong.

I reached out across my social media channels explaining my side affects and asking if anyone had experienced similar. Every comment, even from those who I knew were medically trained, was the same - go to hospital. And yet I resisted this. Instead I called NHS 24 for guidance. After explaining I'd had a 3 mile run in the cold I was dismissed - after all how can there be anything seriously wrong if you managed that while in the same pain?

And yet my instincts were now on fire. For some reason, their dismissal had made me realise with unwavering certainty that I needed to go to A&E. And I needed to go now!

In our local A&E I was met with the same dismissal as I had been on the telephone with NHS 24. I was left waiting for nearly three hours because, 'they forgot I was there' and when I was finally seen the doctor on call referenced the fact I had been running and that he wasn't concerned. I tried to explain that the pain had been there previous to my run and that I have a track record of having a very high pain threshold.

Begrudgingly he used his stethoscope to listen to my chest.

I could see it in his face. That look I'd seen so many times in the past, when a doctor, who only moments previously had been convincing me everything was fine, suddenly starts to doubt themselves.

'I think it might be best if you have a chest x-ray, just to be sure,' he offered calmly.

So, off I went on the familiar journey to the x-ray department in the middle of the night; the cold and dark corridors empty of the usual bustle of the day.

When I returned to A&E for the results the doctor told me that my right lung had fluid on it.

'Oh don't worry,' I casually replied, 'there has been a little bit of fluid there since I was first diagnosed two years ago.'

He exchanged a look with his colleague, who I now realised he had brought in for back up.

'Perhaps you'd like to see your x-ray,' they suggested as they showed me over to the computer screen.

'You can see that your right lung has collapsed and that the surrounding cavity is 75% filled with fluid. It really is a miracle you can walk without getting breathless, let alone run.'

I couldn't believe what I was seeing on the screen. My precious right lung had been squashed up under my right collarbone by the fluid collecting around it. The pain I had been experiencing had been the pressure of my lung being compressed. I was speechless.

The doctors explained that I would need to be admitted to have my lung drained but that since the hospital was so busy, given the additional pressures over the festive period, that I would have a long wait without a bed until a consultant became available. It was already 1am.

I was taken up to the admissions ward two hours later where I was left on a trolley in a corridor. My husband wasn't allowed to wait with me due to the large number of patients sitting in chairs and on the floor already blocking the busy ward. And so I waited alone, in shock and emotional pain at the likeliness that my cancer had returned. I silently pleaded and hoped that it was pneumonia - anything but cancer again.

A Respiratory Issue

Eventually I was admitted to the respiratory ward. Despite my best pleas to be taken to oncology where they knew my medical history, I was told that because I was no longer on active treatment and because they hadn't yet confirmed it was a cancer recurrence that it was 'a respiratory issue'.

Once again I found myself in a new and unfamiliar world. I didn't know any of the team on this ward and they didn't know me. My medical notes are extensive and the staff far from had the time needed to read through them, and so began the frustrating dialogue of me trying to explain my previous treatment while they looked at me with disbelief. It's funny to recall now - although certainly not at the time - the face of my respiratory consultant when I detailed the surgery I'd had. I felt mocked as he observed me with doubt. It wasn't until two days later that he came to apologise because he had finally had a chance to read my notes.

Once on the ward the first port of call was to take a sample of fluid from my lung. I'd had this done before when I was first diagnosed and I was far from keen to go through it again. The memories of the agony I'd experienced previously came back to haunt me and I sent my husband away to spare him my distress. I regretted this decision almost instantly. I now know that in these moments I need him beside me and that is exactly where he wants to be.

When they tried to drain the sample I collapsed. I literally fell over sideways onto the bed and proceeded to have several violent and unrelenting panic attacks. I was alone with two male doctors, topless and terrified. While I lay there shaking and crying they tried several more times to get a sample before the more senior doctor eventually decided I was under too much distress and pain, when my blood pressure began to drop dangerously low.

They had, however, managed to get enough of a sample during this time, passing comment between one another that its appearance was 'consistent with malignant fluid'. Once again I was painfully reminded what it feels like when a member of medical staff forgets you have ears.

Following the sample collection they sent me for another x-ray. This showed that my lung had been punctured during the sample collection. This meant that in addition to the fluid already around my lung, I now had air there too. The worst news about this was being told that I would no longer be able to fly - we had just the day before booked a dream holiday to Thailand.

It's OK to Say No

The next step was to insert a lung drain to remove the build up of fluid. For this procedure I asked my husband to stay by my side. What a difference it made for me, finally, admitting to myself that I didn't have to do this alone. As they inserted the drain I was much calmer, holding his hand and listening to him as he reassured me.

The drain was left in for a few days while they drained 2.5 liters of fluid from my chest cavity. During this time the lab was testing the sample taken to see if the fluid was the result of an infection or a cancer recurrence. However, things were not as straightforward as we had hoped. While the consultants caring for me were convinced I had a cancer recurrence, my temperature and heart rate were elevated in a manner that was consistent with an infection. The lab, however, weren't finding any signs of an infection in the fluid they had taken.

This meant the team had to treat me as if I had both a recurrence *and* an infection. I was given broad-spectrum antibiotics and my chest was carefully monitored with x-rays to check that the fluid was draining and not returning.

I was told that if it was a cancer recurrence that they could drain it but that the fluid would just keep coming back faster and faster until eventually they couldn't drain it anymore. With this in mind they proposed three options: 1. I restart chemotherapy; 2. I have a permanent drain fitted into my lung so that I could drain it myself at home; or 3. They do a procedure called pleurodesis that basically involves putting talc around the lung cavity in order to prolong the time before the fluid recollects.

However, my answer to all three of these suggestions was a clear and firm 'no', much to the dismay of the consultant explaining them to me.

Did I want chemotherapy? No. I had previously had long and detailed conversations with my oncologist explaining that if my cancer were to return that I would decline further, second-line chemotherapy, instead choosing quality of life over quantity. Also, I felt like this was an inappropriate time to even discuss this as an option. Firstly, we hadn't even confirmed that I had a recurrence and secondly, the doctor suggesting it wasn't an oncologist. No thank you, next suggestion please.

Did I want a permanent lung drain? No. I was sure that my oncologist and I had discussed in the past that permanent drains could make patients ineligible for trial treatments. I didn't want to make a potentially life changing decision without first discussing it with my oncologist, who, at that point was on holiday.

Did I want talc put in my lung? NO. Now my response to this was 100%, pure and simple instinct. My body was literally screaming at me not to have this procedure. I can't explain any rational for this but I knew I just had to listen. This wasn't the easiest thing to explain to a consultant that didn't know me and who likely already thought I was nuts for turning down chemotherapy.

I looked into the consultant's eyes and, with compassion, asked 'what would you do in my situation? What would you do if, worst case, next week you were told that your cancer had returned? Would you agree to have any of this treatment? Knowing that it would only extend your life by a matter of months, at the expense of any level of quality of life. Or would you turn it down? And instead try to enjoy some valuable quality of life in the little time you had left?'

They replied with the most honesty I've ever had to that answer. 'No one can answer that unless they are in your exact situation,' they offered, with sadness touching their words.

And that's the reality. None of us know what decision we would make until we are faced with any given scenario for ourselves.

So, what did I agree to?

I agreed to my lung being drained in hospital and then me going home and returning to the hospital in the New Year once my oncologist was back from their festive break. I agreed to informed and collaborative decisions based on ALL available information, rather than making decisions based in a moment. I agreed to a collaboration between respiratory and oncology where I would be monitored by both departments until a treatment plan was made that fit with my values. And, in truth, I think the consultant found it refreshing. After just three days of me being in hospital he was coming to sit in my room at the end of his shift just to see how I was doing. I knew then that we had finally built a collaborative relationship and that I could trust him to have my best interests at heart, even though my wishes didn't fit with the medical norm.

So, a new plan was created. The drain was removed from my lung and I was sent home with an appointment a few weeks later to have another x-ray. I was told that if the x-ray showed that the fluid had returned then we would have no option but to drain it again and put the talc in. If, by some miracle, however, the fluid hadn't returned then they would monitor me until it did. They also booked me in for a CT scan to look for new cancer growth elsewhere in my body and scheduled an appointment between me and my oncologist.

Once again, my only goal was keeping my lungs healthy. Miraculously, that's exactly what I did and just one week after being discharged from hospital I was back teaching my regular yoga class.

Top Tips: Remaining a Person, Not a Patient

When you are in hospital it can be so hard to maintain a sense of self, but it is one of the most important things you can do for your holistic health.

When I am in hospital, even at times when I am critically ill, I still do everything in my personal power to ensure that the team caring for me know the real me, and I also do what I can to get to know them. At the end of the day, we are all just humans trying to live our lives as best we can.

As a result, I'm the patient who brings in her own glass water bottle, rather than use the plastic hospital water jugs provided. It has three crystals inside it and a stick of charcoal too to help filter the water.

I'm the patient who brings her own flask, rather then uses the mugs provided. I also bring my own organic mint tea bags.

I'm the patient who will wear a hospital gown during a medical procedure but then, no matter the pain I'm in, will get dressed as soon as possible afterwards.

I'm the patient who knows that you don't have to wear a gown for a scan, provided you are wearing no metal (for an MRI scan this is because it is basically a giant magnet and for a CT scan this is because it creates 'light beams' in the scan image). Instead I wear leggings and a vest top for my scans, rather than lose my identity in a hospital gown.

I'm the patient who washes and does her hair and puts on a full face of makeup every morning I'm in hospital. Sometimes this means washing my hair in a sink but I still do it. Not out of vanity, but out of a need to express myself as I would outside of the hospital.

I'm the patient who eats dinner with her husband every night (sometimes even a takeaway).

I'm the patient who stores and administers her own medication, rather than waiting for the drug trolley.

I'm the patient who does yoga stretches on or beside her bed each morning, even when I had a chest drain fitted.

I'm the patient who asks a continuous stream of questions until I am satisfied that I know as much as I can about any given situation.

I'm the patient who will take the hand of a stressed and tired nurse and tell them it is not their fault and they do not need to apologise to me.

I'm the patient who will ask a doctor if they need to take a moment to rest in the chair beside my bed before they speak to me.

I'm the patient who sees my team as people and accepts that people aren't perfect, that they make mistakes and that they get emotional and tired too.

I'm the patient who strives, in the same breath, to still be seen as a person too.

I do these things because these are part of my inherent values that make me who I am. I do these things because they are part of my identity and what matters to me. I do these things because, no matter how sick or sore I may be, this is still a part of my life. I do them because it is so important that the people who care for me see 'me' rather than a stage four cancer patient.

What is the result?

I have an active say in my care plan. I am treated with respect. I am listened to. I am visited by members of my medical at the end of their shifts when they should be going home. I am able to get to know my team as if we had met one another out in the 'real world'.

It is so important that we all do whatever we can to maintain our identity. When we are in hospital we become part of a large machine and we can so easily get lost. However, by taking small measures to preserve our independence we not only remind our medical team who we are, we also remind ourselves what matters most to us, what our values are and why we are striving to get well in the first place.

None of the measures I take negatively impact the work of my medical team, and I would never do or recommend anything that does. These incredible people are doing everything they can to preserve the lives of others. Our only job is to help them to see 'us' rather than our medical condition and, in return, for us to see 'them' rather than just another member of staff. In doing so we can connect in ways that are driven by love, not fear, and help to create a more beautiful and magical world.

What can you do when you are in hospital to preserve your identity and to see the identity of the person caring for you?

What patient are you?

The Worst News Confirmed

Going forward I knew that, despite my hopes that it had 'just' been an infection, it was highly likely that the fluid had been the result of a cancer recurrence.

When I finally saw my oncologist she confirmed my fears. My cancer had returned. The fluid on my lungs was malignant. I had two new tumours: one next to my left kidney and one on my right lung. I also had a large mass in my abdomen. By this point I had already been told that if this was the case that my 'mean time' survival would be four to six months.

I took this news very badly at first. I was sad and angry. Very angry. It felt like a much harder blow than my initial diagnosis. Although I had known from day one that my cancer had been incurable, there had always been that tiny piece of silent hope that maybe, just maybe, I would be different and my cancer wouldn't return. It felt like that hope had been shattered. I wasn't different. I was dying.

Mixed, and often negative, emotions are very natural following a cancer recurrence. However, one of the most common emotions is guilt or shame. So often people think that their cancer came back because they did something 'wrong' and that if they had tried a little harder then they would have been cured. This couldn't be further from the truth.

Cancer doesn't come back because of something you did or didn't do. It comes back because it is an insidious disease. Your cancer is not your fault. You did not do anything wrong. Do not ever blame yourself or waste a single second of your beautiful life feeing guilty.

In those first few days following the news I kept myself going by reminding myself of these facts and that, in the words of my medical team, I had everything going for me that I could - I teach yoga, I am young, I have overcome worse, I was running just days before, I eat well and I'm active. I knew then that while I cannot control what will happen, I can control how I react and I can chose to remain filled with love, courage and hope that, whatever the outcome, all will be well. In the meantime the fluid not returning (which would be the most ideal situation) and my body returning to a state of balanced health became my primary focus.

In between check ups with the respiratory team, the

health of my lungs and kidneys was all I could think about. I was determined that when I went for my next x-ray that the fluid wouldn't have returned. My medical team cautiously told me that I needed to prepare myself for further lung drains. However, I became more determined than ever to get my body into a state of ease.

Taking a Deep Breath

In the weeks that followed my discharge from hospital I made many changes in my integrated approach to healing - for easy reference I have detailed these alongside my 'integrated approach' in Part Four of this book. In addition to starting acupuncture, reevaluating the supplements I was already taking, increasing the amount of yoga I was doing, taking more time to rest, starting 'Body Stress Release' and starting medicinal mushrooms under the guidance of an integrated medicine doctor, I also went traveling around Europe by train with my hubby for three weeks without a phone, or a care in the world. We left just six weeks after I was discharged from hospital.

Stepping away from my usual environment and the stress of my situation was invaluable not only for my physical recovery, but also for my emotional recovery as I adjusted to the news that my cancer had returned. Although I was tired, in shock and emotionally drained, that holiday was one of the happiest times in my life and a reminder that we can always chose to enjoy life, even in the face of adversity.

When we returned from our trip I had my first

check-up with the respiratory team. The fluid on my lungs hadn't remained stable. Against all expectations it had reduced. It was the most unexpected and amazing news imaginable.

I will never know for sure whether spending three weeks walking and traveling around France and Italy, eating well and laughing lots helped my lungs to heal, but I am certain of one thing: it did my holistic health more favours than sitting in the house upset ever would have.

At my next appointment, just four months after being first admitted to hospital with a collapsed lung, I was told that there was no fluid or evidence of malignancy on either of my lungs. The consultant explained that this was much better news than he had expected.

'You're clearly a very positive person and it must be working for you' he said, smiling the biggest smile.

I wanted to hug him. I wanted to thank him in some way for trusting that I didn't want chemotherapy, a permanent lung drain or talc put around my lung. I wanted to reward him for listening to me and not my illness. I realised, however, that none of that was needed. The smile on his face, and his look of disbelief and surprise let me know that me still being here was more than enough reward for him.

Still smiling, he discharged me from respiratory, telling me that he wouldn't have to see me again unless my lungs collapsed in the future. At the time of writing this it has been over a year since my cancer returned and my lungs have remained fluid free to this day.

Top Tips: How to Create an Integrated Partnership

Just a week after my oncologist confirmed that my cancer had returned, I asked for another appointment with her. Although I had only just seen her, I was now facing a path of complementary and alternative treatments and I wanted her advice and guidance. I trust her completely and I knew that she was the best person to turn to.

For many cancer patients it can be a nervous moment when you have to discuss what alternatives you are doing (or hoping to do) with your oncologist. Thoughts of doubt can often fill your mind and you may put off the discussion. In fact, many people tell me that they won't tell their oncologist what alternatives they are trying for fear that their oncologist will stop treating them. (A note to any oncologist reading this: please encourage and support your patients to have these discussions).

However, and I can't stress this enough, it is vital that you tell your oncologist *everything* that you are doing - yes even the illegal stuff. Firstly, it enables a relationship built on trust to develop between you both and secondly, some therapies can actually *negatively* impact traditional treatment.

So, please always be honest to save yourself the risk of doing more harm than good when you may already be in a very critical situation. Remember, your oncologist has dedicated their working career to trying to save your life. Think about that. Let that thought sink in for a minute. They are on your team.

Whenever I have discussed complementary therapies with my oncologist, even when I turned down chemotherapy, she did not criticise me, nor did she tell me I was an idiot. Instead, she listened and she offered informed and educated guidance. In fact, her knowledge was fundamental in helping me to navigate the minefield of cancer treatment options including alternatives, trials, private health care and so on. I couldn't have made such informed decisions without her.

CHAPTER 7: GOING PRIVATE

April 2018

Although my lungs were now clear, I knew that my health still wasn't optimal. The cancer in the rest of my body was growing. I was in constant pain from the pressure on my internal organs, caused by the increasing amount of malignant fluid in my abdomen. My cancer was now more aggressive than when I was first diagnosed and the choice to have no treatment was no longer an option if I wanted to keep living.

However, I still stood by my decision to not have chemotherapy and instead asked my oncologist about the option of receiving Avastin - the maintenance drug that I had received alongside my chemotherapy when I was first diagnosed and for almost a year afterwards.

The only problem was, I knew that this drug was no longer available to me on the NHS as I had been given it previously. This was not only because it is an expensive drug, but also because there was no clinical evidence of it being of benefit following eighteen months of treatment.

However, I knew it had worked for me in the past and I was hopeful that it would buy me enough time, and help stabalise my condition long enough, for other treatment options to become available - namely I was waiting for an immunotherapy trial suitable for my cancer type to become available in Scotland. I knew I was taking a risk but I also knew it was what I needed to do if I was going to stay alive.

So, my oncologist put me in touch with a private oncologist in Glasgow with the plan of discussing my suitability for receiving Avastin privately. During this meeting I discovered that 'private' is code for 'really expensive'. Receiving Avastin outwith the NHS would cost me almost £3,000 every three weeks. How could I possibly pay for that?

Before I could even begin to contemplate this, my health took another turn for the worse and I was readmitted to hospital.

Here We Go Again

By April 2018 the amount of malignant fluid (ascites) building up in my abdomen began to affect my quality of life. I was finding it harder and harder to eat and I could no longer do many of the things I loved. Realising that I could put it off no longer, I agreed to a planned hospital admission to have my ascites drained - a procedure, you may remember from earlier in this book, that I am absolutely terrified of.

However, when they tried to drain the ascites it didn't work and my pain and abdominal swelling continued to increase. I tried walking around the ward, various yoga poses, lying on different sides and still nothing. After three days of no fluid draining they decided to remove the drain.

A further scan showed that I now had loculated ascites. This is when the fluid is sectioned off into small pockets and is harder to drain. This is usually caused following extensive abdominal surgery and the resulting scar tissue sectioning off the abdominal space. And so the plan changed, as it so often does in cancer care, and I was scheduled for another drain to be inserted, this time ensuring in was in one of the larger pockets of fluid.

In the meantime I really struggled. Both emotionally and physically I felt myself rapidly decline. I was in loads of pain from the pressure of the ascites and I felt increasingly breathless and distressed.

I'm not going to lie. I found the whole process horrendously tough. I really struggled with the fluid building up, the pain, and the first drain not working. I was terrified that 'this was it' and that life from now on was going to be a slow decline into more pain and suffering.

The hardest part was that no one could tell me

otherwise, because no one knew if a second drain attempt would work.

During this time, I went home on pass and spent some time in nature, meditating and connecting with family and friends. I found myself messaging those close to me and saying 'I need your help' as I finally allowed myself to be truly vulnerable. In doing so I found my inner strength and I felt empowered and held by those I love. As a result, when I returned to the hospital, I felt much calmer.

Two is Better Than One

The doctor performing the procedure had phoned me at home that morning to tell me that he would try to insert two drains, instead of one, so that he could get as much fluid out as possible.

'It's not going to be pleasant, but I'm going to do everything I can for you,' he kindly explained.

When I arrived at theatre I was already heavily sedated. They helped me onto the theatre bed, made sure I was comfortable and even allowed me to listen to my own music. While the doctor set up for the procedure, one nurse gave me a strong sedative through an IV and another nurse held my hand while she stroked my hair. The doctor showed me everything on screen and talked me through the procedure. Aside from a brief outburst of pain and anxiety when they inserted the second drain, I felt close to nothing.

As I was being wheeled out of the theatre room on a trolley, I turned me head to one of the nurses and said 'that was so much better than any of my previous experiences with drains.' 'I know,' she replied with a smile, 'I've read your book.' Isn't it wonderful that when a medical team work together with the care and comfort of their patient at the forefront of their mind, how much less traumatic a medical procedure can be.

With the drains in place they were able to drain two litres of fluid and, although it was uncomfortable having two drains inserted in opposite sides of my abdomen, I felt so much relief as the pressure of the fluid eased.

That night, while I was getting ready for bed, I stood in front of the mirror in the hospital toilet and caught sight of my reflexion. Standing strong and proud, with my scars, colostomy bag and two drain bags attached I realised that two years previous I had been on that same ward, standing in front of the same mirror and crying because I no longer recognised the person I saw before me.

As I looked in the same mirror that evening, however, I couldn't have been more proud of my body for all that it had achieved in the past two years. I couldn't believe how far I had come and the many things I had overcome and achieved along the way. No longer did I see a weak and fragile cancer patient. I saw a warrior. And, with renewed strength and hope, I knew I was ready for the next phase in my journey.

Starting Avastin

In order to start receiving Avastin privately and hopefully prevent the ascites from returning I needed to raise a lot of money. To do this I set up a fundraising page and asked everyone I knew to help. Overnight this page was shared nationally and in the first few weeks it was reported in newspapers, radio shows and TV news.

In an unbelievably short space of time thousands of pounds were raised as friends, family and strangers donated money, held fundraising events and shared my story multiple times.

I am still so unbelievably thankful for everyone who supported this endeavor. The abundant kindness that came to me was remarkable. In just a few days over £5,000 was donated and I was able to afford to start private treatment. I still can't believe the kindness of others using their hard earned and precious money to buy me more time.

Thank you, all of you, for your support. Whether you donated £1 or £2000, I wouldn't be here without you.

Working in collaboration with my new private oncologist, we realised that the cheapest way for me to receive Avastin was through a company called 'Healthcare at Home'. This would involve me paying the private oncologist to monitor me and write my prescriptions for the treatment and then me paying Healthcare at Home to come to my house and administer the Avastin through a drip every three weeks.

This had two benefits. Firstly I would save roughly £1000 per dose by not having the treatment in a private hospital and, secondly I wouldn't have to travel to receive the treatment, meaning I would have more time in the comfort of my own home.

So in April 2018 I started receiving Avastin and things finally began to look up. On the day of my first dose my cancer markers were higher than they had ever been since my initial diagnosis, however, three weeks later, after just one dose of Avastin, they had dropped a massive 60%. This drop was the largest drop I had ever had in a three-week period - even larger than when I was on chemotherapy in 2016.

When I chose to receive Avastin it was hoped that it would slow down or stabalise my cancer. No one had even dared to dream that it might actually reduce it. Having been told at the start of the year that my cancer had returned and that I had a mean time survival of four to six months, this was beyond miraculous news and defiantly worthy of celebrating.

For the next three months I received Avastin at home every three weeks and life was unbelievably joyful. I was back enjoying my life, doing all of the things I loved and all with minimal side affects. My abdominal fluid wasn't returning, my lungs were still clear and my cancer markers were dropping. It felt like a dream come true and I couldn't believe how lucky I was to have been given another chance at life, again.

The Worst Time of My Life

Fast forward a few months to July 2018 and you find a women who is vomiting at regular intervals. Every few days I would have vomiting fits that I was so desperate to ignore that I didn't even tell my dear oncologist. My body was beginning to whisper louder and louder each day and, despite all of the deep inner work I had done over the previous two years, I still chose to ignore it because I was so terrified of what might be wrong.

Whispers, however, as I'd already learnt, soon become screams.

After nearly a month of this I chose to travel to France with my hubby for a two-week holiday. I'd spent the previous few weeks feeling suffocated and exhausted and I felt an overwhelming and desperate need to 'escape'. What I hadn't realised was that what I was so desperate to escape from was within me and, as such, it came along for the ride.

I spent the two-day train journey from Scotland to France in various train toilet cubicles, wedged between the wall and the toilet bowl, not caring that I was sitting on toilet floors, or that my face was resting on a public toilet seat, as my body violently purged in a way I didn't know was possible to survive. By the time we arrived at our accommodation I was weak and exhausted but my body wasn't finished screaming. I spent the next day or so constantly vomiting. By now I wasn't eating at all and even tiny sips of water were causing me to vomit. I remember at one point feeling like I was looking down on my body, my head resting on the toilet seat while I slept. I felt convinced at the time that I had been called to leave my body to allow it the space to heal. When my hubby woke me I had indeed fallen sleep in this way, and had the toilet seat ring mark across the left hand side of my face to prove it. My hubby carried me to bed as I worryingly told him I didn't feel like I was in my body anymore. Unsurprisingly less than 24 hours later I was taken to a French hospital, exhausted, dehydrated and very weak.

The French hospital was an experience I wouldn't rush to repeat. My husband and I were separated so that I could be examined in private and so, while I was taken to a room crammed with other patients lying in beds, he was asked to wait alone in the reception area.

Once separated I was stripped topless - yes completely topless - in front of the other patients and doctors so that my doctor could perform an ECG (heart trace). I was then taken through to another room where they performed various blood tests and fitted me to a drip to give me some now desperately needed fluids. Various doctors and nurses came in to examine me. Each were unconvinced that they were correctly understanding that I have stage four cancer and thought that our collective language barrier was causing confusion.

It was one of the hardest days of my life, made worse by the fact that I wasn't with Ewan who, aside from being a great source of comfort for me, is also far superior at speaking French.

After six hours of being alone in this situation and with my blood now running out of my arm and into the now empty fluid bag because no one was available to change it, I hauled myself out of my bed, went to the nearest doctor and managed a firm 'je veux mon mari', 'I want my husband.' Needless to say, within five minutes Ewan was with me.

A few hours later, I was discharged from hospital with lists of blood results, instructions to have further blood tests done in two days time and a prescription for steroids and antibiotics.

After a few days I made what can only be described as a miraculous recovering, going from the sickest I have ever been to eating my weight in wonderfully delicious fresh, local fish.

When we returned to Scotland the following week I felt fine and dismissed the vomiting experience as nothing more than a virus or infection that I no longer needed to think about. I was wrong.

In August, a few weeks after our return from France, I went away alone to complete a pregnancy yoga teacher training course. Still feeling overwhelmed with life - our holiday having been far from relaxing - I was excited to focus on one of my great passions and to connect with like-minded souls for a three day weekend of training. However, after the first day I found myself unable to move as debilitating pain passed through my body. I battled on, not leaving the course but instead compromising by lying on the floor for the three-day duration. Sometimes stubbornness isn't a virtue.

Unsurprisingly, by the Monday I was admitted to my

local hospital and there began the worst two weeks of my life thus far.

I had a head scan booked that day as part of the ongoing investigation to see what was causing my constant vomiting. So, while there I mentioned the pain I had experienced over the previous weekend and I was advised to visit the colorectal team to see if I had an issue with my stoma or bowel, such as a partial obstruction. This is a common issue with ovarian cancer that can lead to serious, and even fatal, complications and should never be ignored.

So off I went to have my abdomen thoroughly examined once again. The nurse examining me suggested she get a second opinion from a doctor. Again I was examined and, in a single breath, all hopes of it being a quick fix evaporated.

'We need to admit you for surgery,' came his dire decision.

'Why?' I asked, trying and failing to sound even remotely calm.

'We need to see what is going on inside you,' came the blunt and dismissive response.

I tried, in vain, to explain that surgery would prevent me from having any chance of getting on the immunotherapy trial I had so desperately waited for. Thoughts of my only hope slipping through my fingers filled me with fear. I was terrified.

Before I knew what was happening a surgeon had joined the doctor and they were simultaneously trying to convince me that this was the best approach.

I was in shock. They hadn't even done a scan. How could they possibly know this was the best approach?

As they continued to explain I did possibly the rudest, yet most necessary, thing I have ever done to a member of my medical team. I held my hand up to silence them and with more strength than I felt I stated 'I do not consent.'

I knew that there is literally nothing they can do in that situation but to stop and that is exactly what they did, both of them looking completely stunned.

'I want to speak to my oncologist,' I went on. 'I want her to be part of this decision.'

The surgeon started to argue with me, stating that she was a consultant and that I needed surgery imminently. By this point I was hardly listening, all I saw was someone desperate to be right, but not willing to review all of the facts. I knew then that if I was going to have surgery, it certainly wouldn't be her holding the scalpel.

I called my oncologist's office and explained the situation. Within minutes she had called and spoken to the doctor and explained that no I would not be having surgery and that I was to be admitted to the oncology ward. While feeling proud for standing up for myself so assertively I couldn't help but wonder how many patients would have blindly agreed without their oncologist even knowing the surgery was taking place. How much life altering damage is done every day to patients in similar situations?

This is why it is so important for patients - for you! - to be informed and vocal about your health care plan. Of course, it goes without saying that there are emergency situations where surgery is the only option and in those situations the risk of not having surgery outweighs the risk of having it. However only by evaluating *all* of the facts as an informed team, are we able to make safe and sensible decisions.

I knew that surgery would prevent me from getting on the trial I longed to be a part of and so I needed to be sure that it was the best decision in that given moment. Otherwise I would potentially be cutting short my already fragile existence. There was no one I trusted more to make that decision alongside me than my oncologist.

I had abdominal, chest and pelvic CTs as well as various blood tests to try to establish the cause of my vomiting and pain. However, everything kept coming back clear and I was beginning to feel like I was losing my mind. As a precaution I was given two broad-spectrum antibiotics through an IV incase I had a serious infection that hadn't been detected in my bloods. These made my vomiting worse and I began to lose weight rapidly.

A drain was inserted into my abdomen to take samples from a mass that had appeared just above my stoma site on the left hand side of my abdomen. Initially this was thought to be a hernia, but the pain and vomiting was indicating it might be an abscess. However, when tested, the fluid that was drained showed no sign of infection but instead it was high in white blood cells.

When the scans and the fluid results were reviewed together it was confirmed that I had new disease that had spread right across my pelvis. It was massive, filling the entire cavity where my reproductive organs had once resided. I didn't have time to feel devastated. I faced a difficult decision.

One option was to have surgery to remove it as the colorectal team had suggested. The surgery would be as major and potentially as extensive as the operation I'd had previously. During the recovery time I wouldn't be able to have any Avastin as it can slow down wound healing. This delay could, therefore, potentially cause the cancer to return to my lungs and, essentially, for me to die.

The other option was to start an immunotherapy trial. I would be the first UK patient to receive the specific combination of drugs on offer and it was unknown whether they would have any effect on my cancer, but there has a possibility that it could stabilise my condition and prolong my life.

Both options came with a risk and I was completely overwhelmed with it all; to be facing such decisions again, that my cancer was still growing, that I was once again so fragile and weak, that I was still vomiting, that I was in debilitating pain, that I was completely reliant on others, that I was still in hospital.

Not knowing what else to do I was supported to go

home for 24 hours to make a decision. I was disconnected from the IV fluids that had been offering me the little strength I still had and I was switched to oral antibiotics just incase there was also an infection. Now unable to eat or drink at all, I was weaker than I had ever been before. I was given multiple anti-sickness medications to help prevent further vomiting and I was instructed to return to hospital immediately should my vomiting worsen.

In those precious 24 hours I napped in my garden, slept in my bed and created a beautiful healing sanctuary in the space in our home I usually reserve for my clients. All the furniture was removed and I lay on the floor on a bed of cushions and blankets, surrounded by crystals while incense burnt, mantras played and the room glowed in the light of salt lamps. I had created a womb space in which to heal and go inwards.

As I lay there I guided myself on a shamanic journey and found deep revelations in the messages revealed. I journeyed upwards to the upper world where I vividly witnessed a battle between dark and light, I was attacked by snakes and handed a scorpion by a witch in my life on our physical plane and I came back with a clear focus, vision and mission. I knew I was here to be the first to try this new immunotherapy trial. I knew I didn't want surgery. I knew it was going to be ok. I believed in myself and in my purpose and, above all, in the possibility of healing.

I also knew I had to return to hospital, to get my vomiting under control and to get myself strong enough to start treatment.

It was both exciting and terrifying. This was exactly the moment I had been waiting for since my cancer had returned nine months previously.

The only question now, however, was whether my body would still be strong enough to handle it.

CHAPTER 8: TRAIL BLAZING

September 2018

While 'on paper' I appeared eligible for the trial, I still needed to undergo a number of tests to see if I was clinically suitable. This was especially important due to how unwell I had become and the potential that my health was no longer strong enough. Remarkably, however, my body passed every test and on 4th September 2018 I found myself sitting in the research department of the oncology ward, ready to become the first UK patient to start the trial.

The trial, of course, had risks and I had to sign a number of waivers stating that I was aware that, although the three drugs I would be taking were all licensed, that the drug combination hadn't been tested and the associated risks were not clear. Some of the potential risks listed included death and yet I still found myself feeling strangely calm and unafraid.

Since my initial diagnosis I had believed that our body's immune system, or lack there of, is an essential factor in determining whether or not we get cancer. I couldn't, therefore, get my head around why standard treatment involved therapies that reduced our immune system further. As a result I couldn't accept the notion of chemotherapy as a suitable treatment for me. Despite this, when I was first diagnosed in January 2016 I had begrudgingly accepted chemotherapy as my 'only option'.

Immunotherapy, on the other hand, boosts the body's immune system and empowers it to destroy the cancer without destroying the healthy cells.

I knew that this was my chance to support my inner knowing and embrace a completely different therapy that better aligned with my beliefs about how the body heals. So, despite the risks, I felt certain that this was the right choice for me. Sometimes we have to take big risks when something matters this much to us.

A New Approach to Cancer

As part of the trial I was to receive three different drugs. The first was the immunotherapy treatment that would boost my own immune system. This drug is called Durvalumab and was to be administered every four weeks via an IV. The second drug was Avastin. This is the same drug that I had been paying for privately. It is an anti-giogenetic which means it cuts off the blood supply to cancer and helps to prevent it from repairing itself when being destroyed. On the trial I would receive this via an IV every two weeks, rather than every three like when I was paying for it privately. The third drug was Olaporib. This is a parp-inhibitor, which helps to make cancer more visible to the body's immune system and natural defenses. This is especially important because one of the reasons cancer manages to spread around the body is because it creates a shield that hides it and tricks the body into thinking it is a healthy cell - sneaky. This drug was to be taken as tablets twice a day.

Science lesson over, how would this impact my every day life? Well, in the first instance it meant a lot of hospital visits. On the first day I had nearly twenty vials of blood taken for various tests and received Durvalumab and Avastin through a drip. I also started taking Olaporib tablets and was given enough to take home to last me four weeks. I then had to return two weeks later to receive Avastin on its own through a drip. In between times I was also having weekly blood tests to monitor my safety and check that I wasn't having any dangerous, adverse reactions to the treatment.

After four weeks, the cycle restarted with me receiving Durvalumab and Avatsin together again, followed by Avastin on its own two weeks later and so on. I no longer required the weekly blood tests. Instead, my blood was just taken fortnightly when I was in hospital for treatment.

Although I had to be in hospital more often than when I had been receiving chemotherapy in the past, the side affects were nothing in comparison. However, my body was still very weak from months of constant vomiting and I was still experiencing regular episodes of sickness and loss of appetite. For many weeks it continued to be a constant struggle, as I couldn't regain the strength or weight that I had lost.

My lowest point was vomiting over myself while in the bath because I was unable to get out in time. Although I can now look back and smile, at the time I was so close to giving up and so terrified that this was all I could hope for in the future. If you've been in this dark place, or find yourself there now, please remember that you are not alone. There are many of us there with you.

The Results

After eight weeks on the trial I had my first scan to see if this new tretament was being affective. I had been told, at the time of starting the trial, that it was hoped that the trial would stabilise my disease and stop it growing. It was also explained that people in similar trials appear to have one of two different reactions to treatment. Either they don't respond to treatment and their cancer spreads, or they respond positively very quickly and they have a sustained response. I was obviously hopeful to be a member of the latter group.

Going for my scan I was overwhelmed. I knew the significance of this scan was far greater than any scan I'd had previously. If this scan showed progression (i.e. that my cancer had grown or spread) then I would be taken off of the trail and there would be no treatment options for me, unless I reconsidered my view on chemotherapy - which I wouldn't. If the scan, on the other hand, showed a reduction or slowing down of my cancer then I would know that I was receiving a drug that could positively impact the future of ovarian cancer treatment and that would obviously be amazing! I remained positive.

Nothing, however, could have prepared me for the results. My cancer had shrunk significantly. After just eight weeks of treatment, I was facing a very different situation from the one I had been in before. In the space of ten months, I had gone from my cancer returning, to being told I had a dire prognosis, to multiple unplanned admissions, to fundraising and paying for private treatment, to months of vomiting and weakness as my cancer spread, to taking the risk and starting a trial I believed in greatly, to the best news imaginable. The contrast was overwhelming and for many weeks I would have outbursts of tears as the reality of my situation sunk in. I couldn't believe how lucky I was to not only still be alive, but to be feeling so incredible.

I've now been on the trial for eighteen weeks. My sixteen week scan on Christmas Eve 2018 showed that my cancer is stable and my most recent blood tests show that my cancer markers are not only in healthy range, they are the lowest they have been in two years. Remarkable!

Today

This week marks ten years since Ewan and I had our first date, the three-year anniversary of my cancer diagnosis and my eldest sister's wedding. There were many moments over the past year where I didn't think I would make this special week. More than several times my medical team heard the world 'just get me to my sister's wedding'. Today, as I write these words, I am filled with complete gratitude not only for the support of my medical team, but for all those who helped pay for the private treatment that allowed me to stay alive until I started the trial. Above all I am unbelievably grateful for the healing power that I found within me. The same healing power, I believe, is within each of us.

My life hasn't been easy but I wouldn't change a single moment of the bad because it not only makes me value the good, but I now know what it feels like to value every single second of my life and to not take a single moment for granted. Above all, I know that when I walk down the aisle on my sister's wedding day it will be one of the happiest moments of my life.

What the Future Holds

Recently I woke from a very vivid dream with tears in my eyes.

In my dream, someone had stood before me and said 'I can take it all away, I can make it so you never had terminal cancer.'

I remained silent as they went on 'You would never have had the chemotherapy; your hair would still be intact and you never would have suffered the distress it caused you. Your surgery wouldn't have happened; your scars would vanish, your colostomy wouldn't exist and the trauma you experienced would disappear from your mind.'

In my dream I finally muttered, 'would I remember

the lessons?'

'Only if you wanted to' they replied.

'Would I be teaching yoga?' I asked, slightly bewildered.

'No, you would still be in your previous job.'

Then, somewhere between the dream and awakening I began to think about what this would mean.

I would never have taught a single child yoga and, as a result, I would never have witnessed the magic that happens when a child is gifted the ability to self sooth, or the wonder in their eyes when they learn about chakras, or the softening of their spirit as I teach them the mantra of 'I am kind, I am loved, I am safe, I am enough.'

I would have never made the friends I have through cancer and, as a result, so many people I cherish deeply would still be strangers.

I never would have written this book or personally had the honour of connecting with thousands of people as they go through their own cancer journey.

I never would have shared the tears and felt the connection when people write to me about a loved one passing away from cancer, or the joy when I am told someone has survived against all the odds.

I wouldn't have known what it's like to have everything I thought was 'me' stripped away to leave the raw reality upon which I could rebuild the warrior I have become.

I never would have met, nor witnessed, the incredible medical staff who I have had the absolute privileged of receiving care from. My oncologist, my surgeons, the nurses (oh the wonderful nurses), the porters, the cleaning staff, the volunteers and the doctors would all have remained strangers and I would never know what it is like to witness, nor receive, the passionate, person-centred care that they offer.

I wouldn't place the value I do on time away with my hubby, on days with my family or on adventures with friends. Instead, perhaps, I would have kept working long days and commuting long hours, unaware that my precious life was slipping past me in a blur.

I wouldn't have handed out a single random act of kindness and, sadly, I wouldn't have connected with the lives and stories of so many beautiful strangers, some of whom have become dear friends and, all of whom, have taught me some of the most valuable lessons in life.

And, in that beautiful moment, I realised something.

I wouldn't trade a single second of my diagnosis, of my treatment, of my surgery or of my recovery if it meant that I would miss out on any of the wonderful gifts it had brought me.

In that moment I knew that, while my cancer may never be cured, I can say now, without a shadow of doubt, that I am completely 'healed' in every sense of the word and that is the greatest gift of all.

I don't know what the future holds for me. I will be on the trial for as long as it continues to be effective, with scans every eight weeks to check what my cancer is doing. But, in the meantime I will continue to enjoy each day, each moment, each breath and I will remain optimistic about the possibility of healing. That's all any of us can do.

Top Tips: Trial Treatments

Please note - suitability for a trial is not just a simple case of having a certain type of cancer (i.e. ovarian cancer). It is also about what grade your cancer is, what stage it is, what your performance factor is, your genetic composition, when you last had treatment and what that treatment was, your blood results, the size and spread of your tumours, what treatment they have responded to in the past, and so much more. I know, first hand, how frustrating it can be to see someone else with 'the same' diagnosis as you get treatment that you can't. I've felt the pain of my BRCA positive ovarian sisters getting drugs that prolonged their life that I couldn't get because I am BRCA negative.

This was one of the main reasons why I knew that I had to say yes to the trial I am now on, despite the risks; not just for me but so that one day, if the drugs prove effective, it will be available for other women and more people will get longer with their sisters, mothers, daughters, aunts, wives, girlfriends, cousins, friends, nieces, grandmothers.

I said when I was diagnosed that if my situation saved the life of just one other woman then it would all be worth it, and I meant it.

If you would like to receive trial treatment then you must consult your oncologist. There are new trials opening all of the time and you never know when one you are eligible for may come along.

When I was first diagnosed I wasn't eligible for any trials. In fact it took nearly three years before I got on a trial. However, in the meantime I never stopped asking my oncologist and I trusted that one day there would be one just right for me.

PART FOUR

AWAKENING YOUR HEALING POWER

CHAPTER 9: AN INTEGRATED APPROACH

Disclaimer - I want to reiterate a very important point. I am not a medical doctor and I have no medical training. I have not written this book to encourage you to make any particular lifestyle changes but rather to provide information on what worked for me. In any case, it would be irresponsible to recommend anyone to take any of the steps I have, as our incredible bodies all respond in very different ways. In all honestly, the most important change I made following my cancer diagnosis was to no longer take life too seriously. Instead, I simply embrace the fact that today I am alive and, in doing so, I now live a life full of joy, hope and pleasure.

Ultimately, the only advice you should take from my protocol, or anyone else's for that matter, is to trust your instinct and do what is right for you.

I hope the following will serve to prompt you as you start to explore some of the wonderful things you can do to awaken your healing power within.

As an active member of the 'cancer community' I recognise that the topic of treatment is not entirely straightforward. From a conventional point of view, cancer patients are offered a range of treatments broadly categorised under surgery, chemotherapy and radiotherapy. The array of drugs available is, of course, constantly changing as new research studies are conducted. As a result, many cancers are now also managed through the use of 'maintenance' drugs such as Avastin for Ovarian Cancer and Tamoxifen for Breast Cancer.

From a complementary treatment point of view there is a wealth of information on a range of therapies and lifestyle changes available for the curious cancer warrior. As a researcher, the examination and evaluation of these treatments is obviously of great importance to me. However, I have also come to understand that the key to any cancer treatment plan - or any health plan for that matter - is that you must trust your instinct and go down whatever route feels right for you. Your choices should be met with compassion and support not only from your loved ones but also from those with an active role in your care plan, be it your oncologist or your shaman! Most importantly you should be free to change your mind at any stage without judgement or explanation. When it comes to your health there is no wrong option other than going against what your heart tells you. This, understandably, can be hard for those who are supporting a loved one with cancer, particularly if the 'patient' declines the treatment (conventional or otherwise) being suggested by the well-meaning supporter. Respect is key here. While it is, of course, okay to offer options it is not okay to strongly inflict personal views or take offence if a cancer warrior chooses a different path from that being suggested.

Personally I took an integrated approach to my healthcare plan, choosing to have a range of both conventional and complementary treatment therapies.

By the time I received my diagnosis, my cancer had spread throughout my abdomen and into my chest cavity. Medically speaking my diagnosis was stage four B. Cancer was everywhere.

In the fateful first two days following my diagnosis I was told that I needed to start treatment imminently in order to preserve my life. My prognosis wasn't great. Fear fed my every decision.

Having been told that my condition was likely inoperable and that chemotherapy would be administered in order to 'manage my symptoms' I thought this was my only choice. My thinking was informed by everything society and the media had ever told me about cancer. The fact that we must kill cancer is drilled into our minds. Indeed, the words 'cancer' and 'fight' often go hand in hand as patients are expected to burn, poison or cut the tumours and cancerous cells from their bodies.

So, led by this information, overwhelmed by fear and with no clue at that stage that other options may exist, I agreed to conventional treatment and started chemotherapy.

However, in the weeks that followed, I began to conduct my own extensive research. While my body underwent the brutality of conventional cancer treatments, I focused my mind on researching the treatment and underlying causes of cancer. I was driven by the fact that, despite being young, active and healthy, I had been diagnosed with non-genetic, late stage, aggressive cancer. The more I read, the more unsettled I became. A question kept coming to my mind that seemed to fit with everything I was reading: 'what if cancer is just a symptom of 'dis-ease'?'

I realised that if I were to have any chance of healing then my health should be viewed holistically. So I began developing my personal healing journey by looking not at the cancer in my body, but at the 'dis-ease' in my environment, mind, body and spirit. The deeper I explored, the more I realised that I wasn't as healthy as I thought. Everyday practices in modern Western society had left my body in a state of 'dis-ease'. Stress, anxiety, suppressed emotional and physical traumas and processed foods plagued my immune system. It was this 'dis-ease' that I began to believe caused my body's cancer cells to take over. After all, evidence shows that we all have cancer cells in our body. It is when our immune system stops identifying cancer cells and they begin to take over that an issue arises. As a result, it became my firm belief that by putting my body back into a state of ease that I would be able to return myself to wholeness and heal my life. I needed to start making changes and fast!

Through the extensive changes I made something wonderful started to happen. I began to feel happier and healthier than I ever thought possible, regardless of what cancer was doing inside my incredible body.

Having done extensive research, I now strongly believe that while conventional treatment is impeccable at treating the symptoms of cancer (and, indeed, many other modern illnesses) it is sadly lacking at treating the all important cause of the 'dis-ease' that led to the cancer diagnosis in the first place. This is where, I believe, complementary therapies are able to play a wonderful role at enabling a person to heal.

For this reason I have chosen to discuss these forms of treatment entirely separately from all of my medical treatment. While they go hand in hand and I am more than certain I wouldn't be alive if it weren't for my integrated approach, they are, in fact, treating very different aspects of the whole person. In short, I believe, that while conventional treatment stopped me dying, it is complementary treatments that have kept me alive.

The clearest analogy I have for this came to me when in October 2016 (for the first time ever) I got very badly sunburnt. Those of you who have been sunburnt before know that, naturally, the first response is to get out of the sun. That evening you will likely have a cold shower and apply some soothing cream (hopefully a mix of coconut oil and jojoba oil and no chemical filled nasties like aftersun). The next day, if you have any sense, you won't be found sunbathing. Instead you will sit in the shade or cover your skin with some protective clothing.

In this scenario you instinctively know that both the cause and the symptom need treated in harmony. Here the cause is too long in the sun and the resulting symptom is sunburn. You know that you must treat the symptom to relieve your discomfort but that you must also treat the cause in order to prevent your situation from worsening. You wouldn't, for instance, continue to sit in the sun day after day getting more and more burnt to the point of your body becoming covered in agonising blisters with the hope that a cold shower each evening would resolve the problem? Well, if you would then, let's be honest, this probably isn't the book for you.

So, why is cancer treatment any different? Why do we think that treating the symptom (i.e. the cancer) and not finding and treating the cause (i.e. the 'dis-ease') will resolve the situation long term?

With this mindset being so prevalent in Western culture it is no wonder to me that cancer recurrence rates are so high. Research indicated that the warriors who take a holistic and integrated approach to their treatment plan have a higher survival rate than those who only have conventional treatment (surgery, chemotherapy and/or radiotherapy) without making any lifestyle changes.

Based on this, alongside my own personal experience, it is my strong belief that if we are to see more and more warriors not just living with their cancer but thriving, then it is imperative that we stop treating the symptoms alone. Instead we must focus our energy on finding and treating the cause to help ensure the best chance of survival for more people with cancer.

The Difference Between Being Healed and Being Cured

Many cancer warriors, in particular those with late

stage or incurable cancer, spend precious time in desperate search of the 'cure'; the perfect protocol that will make their cancer disappear. I can, of course, relate to this desperation. However, I have also found great peace in letting it go. I now raise the question 'what if it is more important that we seek to be healed rather than cured?' Now, you may be asking 'what is the difference?' Well, in my opinion, the difference is huge.

To be healed is to return to wholeness. It is to look deeply at every aspect of our lives and see where dis-ease lingers. It is to ask what environmental, physical, emotional and/or spiritual imbalances led to an accumulation of this dis-ease manifesting as cancer (or any other modern illness) within our physical body.

To be cured, on the other hand, is to remove the cancer from our body and hope that it doesn't return. Of course a cure would be wonderful but not at the expense of healing. All too often cancer warriors (and other patients) can get caught up on being cured without using it as a platform to explore and improve their lives.

I don't know if embracing an integrated approach to health will ever cure my cancer but one thing is for sure; it healed my fear of cancer and taught me how to live again. Perhaps that is more important.

Stop The War on Cancer

One thing that countless medical professionals and researchers agree is that every person has cancer cells in their body at any given point. Yes. Everyone.

A cancer cell is just a normal cell that didn't do what it was supposed to. It may have divided more than it should have for instance. This error is happening every single day in each and every one of us.

In a healthy person the body detects this error and removes the cell or rectifies the issue. This is done because they have a strong immune system that is doing its job at keeping their body healthy and their cells working effectively. Problem solved.

The difference between us cancer warriors and someone who doesn't have a cancer diagnosis however is that our immune system didn't notice the first error, or the second, or the third and so on. Instead, our bodies treated our misbehaving cells the same as our healthy cells. Instead of being removed they were fed and encouraged to grow. Not only that, but they were then helped to move around our bodies by our blood and healthy cells.

As the number of these cells increased, the effectiveness of our immune system continued to decrease as it became further compromised by these misbehaving cells. As a result, our bodies became less and less able to detect these cells and, before we knew it, we had cancer. All because our body didn't detect that first cell that got things wrong.

So, biology lesson over, what does this mean?

Firstly, it means that cancer is not an external source; it is created by our bodies; it is fed by our bodies; and it is spread by our bodies. Most importantly, it is part of our bodies!

When we say we are fighting our cancer, we are declaring a war on ourselves. What a horrible way to live.

So if we don't fight what do we do?

Now, while cancer itself is not an external source, I believe that the factor(s) that contributed to the lowered immune system that didn't detect that first rogue cell is. For some, these external factors may include, for example, smoking, alcohol, pesticides, toxins, stress, illness and so on. In my case, as a non-smoker, minimal drinker and healthy eater, I think my factors ran deep and included emotional stress and anxiety, environmental toxins, illness and pesticides.

So, since my diagnosis, instead of fighting my cancer, as society suggests - which would only create anger, stress and anxiety and further toxify my immune system - I have instead focused on rebuilding my health and nurturing my body, mind and spirit as a peaceful warrior. And, as crazy as it may seem, I send love to each and every one of my cells (even the misbehaving ones) every day. I love my body for the incredible things it has endured and survived and for the life it gives me.

I don't think 'fighting' is the right approach to heal from cancer. Instead, I want to promote the healing of my fellow warrior's minds, bodies and spirits.

Trying to fight cancer with anger, resentment and hate only causes us to miss the point and the incredible value that cancer can bring if we'd only just stop, take a breath and listen.

I'm not saying I think this approach will cure our cancer but it will certainly heal our minds, bodies, and spirits of dis-ease. If nothing else, your life will become more peaceful as a result because you will no longer live with the constant anger that so many warriors do towards their cancer and their bodies. I would rather live out my days with this approach to life rather than by fighting with my body and myself.

Take note of the language you use around cancer. I know it may not be easy to start sending love to your cancer, but could you begin, at the very least, by not sending it any more hate?

Just imagine how lighter and freer your life would become if you stopped focusing all of your negative energy on your cancer and instead just let it go.

It feels great doesn't it?

CHAPTER 10: MIND

When facing a cancer diagnosis it can seem natural to jump to the physical changes that you may wish to make in order to heal yourself. However, health must be viewed holistically and therefore it is just as important, if not more so, to also explore your emotional and mental health.

For this reason I have chosen to start this part of the book with my personal journey through emotional healing, during which I had to face some often painful issues from my past that I had previously ignored and buried deep.

Reflecting on all that I learnt through this process, it is no longer surprising to me that ovarian cancer (as well as breast cancer) is often associated with women who have experienced an emotional trauma from a partner. In fact, if we are to take a moment to look at chakras, Eastern medicine indicates that suppressed emotions are stored in the sacral or heart chakras. These correspond directly with the reproductive or sexual organs (sacral chakra) and the chest area (heart chakra). As a result, dealing with my emotional health was at the forefront of my healing journey.

Reduce Stress

There is a prevalent view in society that we need to be stressed; that we are not reaching our true potential unless we are stretched so thinly that our health starts to suffer. Well I am here to tell you that this is utter bullshit. Leading a happy and fulfilling life doesn't need to be stressful. In fact, if anything, it should be far from stressful. It should make you feel amazing!

Firstly, there is a huge difference between stress and passion. I am probably busier now than I was before my diagnosis, however, I am no longer in a state of stress. Instead I am driven by a passion to follow my dreams. Sometimes that means I work over the weekend or in the evenings but it no longer matters because I now love what I do. Therein lies the difference. If it makes you happy doing what you do then go for it. You have found your passion.

In contrast, however, if what you do - whether it be your job, hobbies, social commitments and so on - makes you miserable, makes you feel less of yourself, or drains you, then something has to change. If not, then you will be placing your body in a prolonged state of stress and it does you no good.

I remember during my second chemotherapy dose I

met an incredible young woman who sadly is no longer with us. She shared my zest for life and soon we were chatting like old friends. It turned out that she also had stage four cancer. Hers, however, was oesophageal cancer. We joked that given that prior to our diagnoses neither of us had smoked, we both rarely drank and we were keen exercisers who ate healthily, it must have been stress that caused our cancer. 'You'd be surprised' one of the chemo nurses announced, 'we see a lot of 'healthy' stressed people in here.'

Could it be that stress creates too much dis-ease in our bodies, leaving them unable to identify cancer cells and unable to heal? I certainly started to wonder what the stress in my life had been doing to my body.

I began to realise that not only was I stressed about my job, about achieving the best results in my career, but I was also stressed about what other people thought about me, about being the 'perfect' friend, the 'perfect' wife. I was also stressed about our home looking 'perfect' all of the time. I had been stressed about whether or not we had children and, if we had, I'm sure I would have been stressed about what kind of parent I was. I got stressed about how I looked, what I weighed and what I wore. The list was endless.

As I looked around me I realised that I wasn't alone. Almost everyone I knew was living with high levels of stress in their lives.

It took some time but I have let all of that shit go. I left my long sought after job and, admittedly, after months of caring what other people would think about this decision it turns out that no one cared. As long as I was happy not one single person batted an eyelid. I also stopped caring what my house looks like. I am very house-proud and I used to hate when people saw my house looking anything less than 'perfect' but then I realised that no one has a perfect home. Now I don't mind if there is washing hanging up to dry or dishes in the sink when a friend pops by. After all, they are there because they want to see me, not to critique how tidy my home is. And, if that isn't the case, are they really that good a friend after all?

Take a look at all of the self-inflicted stress in your life and see what you can let go of. At the end of the day, if it no longer serves you then it's time to say goodbye.

Let Go of Deep Seated Negative Emotions

There is increasing evidence that cancer starts following a significant trauma. Interestingly, many Eastern medicine practices report that emotional trauma sits in our lungs. It is here that, Japanese medicine shows, our grief and fear is stored. For this reason when I heard that my cancer had spread to my right lung I began to question whether I had issues with unresolved traumas.

I reflected on this in the weeks following my diagnosis. Which trauma in my past had been the significant one? Was it the physically abusive relationship I'd endured with an ex partner for three years? Doing a PhD? Losing loved ones? Witnessing a violent attack in which the victim was hospitalised, unconscious? What constitutes a 'significant' trauma?

For years I had subconsciously been carrying around a lot of physical and emotional traumas, each negatively affecting my health over a prolonged period of time. Work needed to be done if I were to heal myself.

In the following months, I read a lot about dealing with traumas. One process in particular, detailed in 'Radical Remissions' by Dr Kelly Turner, resonated with me the most deeply. This involved writing down everything about the traumas and then burning the paper. It seemed like an easy place to start and so I began straight away. Unknowingly this took me on an emotional journey. Hours later I was still detailing all of the hurt I'd been carrying as the tears flowed down my checks.

In particular, coming to terms with living in an abusive relationship with my ex partner was one of the largest emotional traumas I had to come to terms with. Unexpectedly, I was not just reliving the pain of the time he smashed my head against a mirror, threw me to the floor and held me by the throat while he spat in my face, or the time he broke down a door to try to choke me, to name a few. I was also dealing with the emotional scars of the years of lying to the people I loved as I tried to cover up these actions. The secrets, the lies and the denial, it seemed, had emotionally scarred me much more deeply than any physical wound he could have inflicted.

After years of living in fear I realised that I was no longer scared of him. I was, however, still deeply angry that he had made me deceive others in order to protect him. So, as part of my emotional recovery, I told people what had happened and, in doing so, I removed the chains that had bound my spirit for almost a decade. I felt instantly lighter and more connected to those I love and who love me.

I had carried the weight of an abusive relationship around with me for so long that when it finally lifted I couldn't believe how wonderful I felt. It took over a year of deep work at an emotional level to remove nearly ten years of emotions I had buried deep in my body. It wasn't easy but it was worth it. All the hurt, the anger and the fear had shifted. I'd spent years hating my abuser. The very thought of him had filled me with the darkest of emotions. Now the hate and fear was going. Instead, whenever I thought of him I felt nothing. I had reached a state of peace. It was incredibly empowering.

However, my journey of dealing with this phase in my life didn't end there. I wanted to reach a stage where I was able to feel the same nothingness towards his actions. I longed to reach a state of peace about my experience and this challenging period in my life. This took a lot of time and was often extremely painful. In a similar approach to not fighting my cancer, I stopped sending hate and fear out towards my ex partner. Each day, following my meditation, I would send forgiveness not because I condoned his actions (far from it) but because I needed internal peace for myself. It was the most unnatural thing I had ever done. Over time, however, it got easier and in the months that followed I felt much more at ease.

Some time later I realised that I still needed to do further work to completely heal from this trauma in my life. I realised that while I had removed the fear and anger I hadn't forgiven myself and, as a result, I hadn't released the shame and self-judgment I still carried from living in an abusive relationship. As soon as I forgave myself I became whole again. I realised that I had continued to victimise myself for many years after being subjected to his actions and that this prolonged suffering had been my own choice. I took this knowledge and deep understanding and applied it to other aspects of my life, namely my cancer diagnosis. I realised that I was no longer willing to be a victim of any external circumstances. As a result I didn't want to be labelled as a cancer patient or even a cancer survivor but instead just as a woman living an incredible and fulfilling life.

Working through emotional traumas is one of the hardest things I think anyone can do, but it is also one of the most rewarding. If this part of my story resonates with you then I encourage you to distance yourself from the situation and to work on healing yourself on an emotional level. Abuse, whether emotional or physical, is never acceptable and there is never an excuse. Value yourself enough to know that you are worth more than the negative actions of another human. Your life is in your hands and you can take back control.

If you want to do the exercise I did to help you process trauma or negative feelings in your life then set aside a few hours when you won't be disturbed. Then take a pen and paper and write down everything that's happened in your life that created a negative feeling. Go as far back as you can remember and really think about what it was in each scenario that affected you. Write down everything. This is an emotional process so please take your time. Once you have finished going over everything simply burn the pieces of paper (ideally on the night of a full moon) and be done with it. You will feel much lighter for having let all of this negativity go back to its source.

Avoid Negative People

We all have people in our life that lower our mood or drain us emotionally when we are in their company. My advice is simple; get them out of your life. When you are on a healing journey there is nothing more draining that the negativity of someone else. Personally, I have now distanced myself from anyone who constantly moaned about their life without making attempts to change it, as well as anyone who was overly depressed about my diagnosis to the point that they were draining my own positivity. I'm not suggesting that this should be used as an excuse to be cruel or unkind; rather I am encouraging you to take note of how you feel when you are around the people in your life.

Pay attention to who energises you and who drains you and make a conscious effort to spend more time with the former. Once I started to pay attention to how I physically felt in the presence of the people in my life I was surprised to notice that while I left some people's company feeling full of life and vitality, others would leave me feeling drained and requiring a few hours (sometimes days) to recharge. I have since parted ways with some of these people in a respectful manner, recognising that we were not supporting one another.

While I appreciate that this can be a hard decision to make, for me it was essential in increasing the value I get out of my social activities. We can't be expected to carry everyone else all of the time. At the end of the day we are each responsible for our own lives and our own personal health.

All this said, we should also take note of how we make other people feel. Are we constantly moaning about our diagnosis and not listening to what is happening in the lives of our loved ones? Relationships work two ways and it is important to not let a health diagnosis, or any other drama in our lives, become the forefront of our connection with others.

Some of my greatest friendships are now with the people that never mention my diagnosis in the day to day, instead saving its reference only for when I have hospital appointments. Remember you were a friend before you were a cancer warrior. Don't over identify or label yourself with your diagnosis. You are so much more than that.

Healing Time in Nature

I truly believe that spending time in nature is healing. Humans are mammals, and like other mammals on the planet we are meant to spend time outdoors in the elements and surrounded by nature. There are countless studies that show, for instance, that people in hospital with a view of an outdoor, green space heal faster than those without a view. Even the presence of a green plant in a hospital room can speed up healing time.

Similarly there is evidence that office workers with a

view of nature or a plant in their office are able to maintain extended periods of concentration. As for children, the benefits of nature are extensive. I wrote my PhD on how time in the outdoors is essential for children. Modern life, however, seems to be doing everything it can to disconnect us from nature.

It is surprising for me to realise on reflection, that in the lead up to my diagnosis I was spending very little time in nature or even outdoors. In fact, aside from walking to and from a train station, I was never outside, ever. Now, however, I have reconnected with the natural world and I am so grateful for it.

I spend a minimum of two hours outside each day. This is the length of time reported as being required if our immune system is to benefit from the natural world. During this time I eat meals, I sit and meditate and sometimes I do yoga.

Above all, each and every day I go for a walk through our nearby woods and connecting with the trees. There is something so magical about the feeling I get when in the presence of trees. The air feels so much cleaner and cooler as it enters my lungs. Often I will take off my shoes and walk barefoot or embrace a tree in my arms. This, in case you are interested, is known as 'grounding' and is said to return the human body back to its natural frequency. The Earth's field has a normal lower frequency range of 7.8 Hz, which is the same frequency as the Alpha and Theta waves in our brains. These brain waves are the ones we tune into when we are in a state of relaxation and meditation.

It is believed that by connecting with the Earth and 'grounding', that we are able to induce this mental state more easily and help our body to return to a state of harmony. Don't believe me? Go and walk on some grass without any shoes on and feel the calming affect for yourself. It's great after a busy day or when you need to recharge. It is also possible to create this feeling through the visualisation of nature before or after a period of meditation or simply by bringing some crystals or plants into your home.

Aside from all of the emotional benefits that nature and being outdoors can bring to our bodies, there are also, obviously, countless physical benefits. When I was diagnosed, the pain in my chest and fluid on my right lung meant that I was unable to walk 50 metres. However, following my second dose of chemotherapy, we welcomed a rescue dog into our home and everything changed. He ensured that every day, even when I wasn't feeling well enough, I got up early and went outside. As a result, each morning, before I could do anything else, I was filling my lungs with fresh oxygen. Each day, regardless of the weather, I would go for a walk. Within the space of a few months I was walking three miles a day.

When our beautiful dog passed away in December 2016, I still maintained my daily walks alone until the arrival of our puppy, Ozzy, in September 2018 who now ensures I am constantly outside!

So, no matter how you are feeling, get up and go outside and breathe in that beautiful fresh air. Try your hardest to go for a walk, however small, and build it up slowly.

Pleasure, Joy and Laughter

There is no point in releasing all of your negative emotions if you aren't going to start refilling your life with positive ones. Above all other changes that you may or may not make on your journey to wholeness, the most important thing you can do is to start enjoying your life. Really start to live the life you have always wanted. Don't wait until tomorrow. Do it now.

So many of us live our lives waiting for happiness to find us but in reality we have to create happiness for ourselves. There are no second chances. This, today, is our one and only life. It's up to us to grab it and get out of it what we truly desire.

Laughter and pleasure are both reported as helping with countless medical concerns such as pain and anxiety. They also both help boost your immune system, which we now know is essential following a cancer diagnosis, and also plays a massive role in preventing it in the first place.

So, what makes you happy? When was the last time you had a deep, belly laugh? What gives you pleasure?

In the lead up to, and while recovering from, my surgery I made lists of all of the things that mattered to me and gave me joy. I really started to think about what I wanted from life and then I made it happen. I now fill my days with love and laughter and I've never felt more alive.

Above all I now prioritise time for self-care, taking the time in each day to do things that rejuvenate me such as a walk in nature, a hot bath, reading a good book or doing yoga.

All too often we put ourselves at the bottom of our ever growing 'to do' lists. However our health must come first.

Take some time to think about what makes you happy, write a list and go and do more of that stuff! Your mind, and your body, will thank you for it.

Top Tips - Making Your Mind Healthier

1. Let go of any self-inflicted stress in your life.

2. Give yourself time and space to work through negative emotions.

3. Seek professional help from a therapist to support you to work through past traumas.

4. Avoid negative people in your life.

5. Connect with more positive people.

6. Spend more time in nature.

7. Do more of what makes you laugh.

8. Walk barefoot on some grass.

9. Write a list of all of the things that bring you joy. Do some of them.

10. Meditate.

CHAPTER 11: ENVIRONMENT

Since my diagnosis I have read extensively about all of the toxins we are unknowingly exposed to in our homes and daily lives. These range from chemicals in our tap water, toxins in our cleaning products and parabens in our beauty products. This was of particular interest to me after I became increasingly aware that cancer is caused by a lowered immune system, often associated with 'toxic' lifestyle choices. As a regular exerciser, who had never smoked and rarely drank alcohol I began to question what other toxins I'd been exposed to that I hadn't even considered.

I was shocked at what I discovered. I had no idea how many toxins are commonplace within the modern household. The more I researched the more shocked I became until one day I reached tipping point. I went round my house with a cardboard box and filled it with every cleaning and beauty product I owned and took them to the dump. These ranged from kitchen sprays to shampoos to makeup to washing up liquid. Each product contained countless chemicals that I no longer wished to expose my delicate body to. Next I used my newfound knowledge to buy and make natural alternatives that were just as effective, and often cheaper, than those that I had disposed of.

In this chapter I have provided an overview of some of the swaps I made to the common products found in my home environment, as well as some of the simple recipes I now use to make my own products.

This list is not exhaustive a there continues to be ongoing new evidence about the toxins we are unwillingly exposed to in everyday life. However, it serves as a starting point for change and discussion.

Candles

There is a mixed debate on candles. Many reports view them as carcinogens, while others say that natural candles, such as those made with beeswax, are fine to use. I love candles so this was a hard choice for me but I now never use them in our home.

Instead I purchased a number of electronic aromatherapy oil diffusers that I have positioned in various rooms. These work with water and a few drops of essential oil. Electricity heats the mixture to release a scented steam that will fill your home with a beautiful aroma. These also have the added bonus of releasing the therapeutic benefits of the aromatherapy oil that you choose. My personal preferences are frankincense, ylang ylang and geranium.

Plastics

Everywhere you look in modern society there are plastics. Our food is wrapped in plastic, our clothes are made from plastic, our water is stored in plastic, children's toys are made from plastic and even our carpets contain plastics. Not only are these detrimental to the natural environment, they are also reported as creating havoc with our health and, in particular, our hormones. Having not just any cancer, but a hormonal cancer, I knew plastics had to go. Straight away I disposed of all of the plastic food containers and bowls in our home, replacing them with glass alternatives. I now only store my food in glassware. This doesn't have to be expensive; for instance, I've found that glass jars make great food containers. I even purchased a glass water bottle to replace my plastic one.

I also try to only buy food that is either loose or packaged in paper or glass. Where this is not possible, and I have to buy food in plastic, I repackage it in glass as soon as I am home.

Water

It surprised me to discover that not only is all tap water treated with a number of chemicals, including chlorine and fluoride, but that it is also considered 'safe' for drinking even if it contains some human faeces. You can even visit your local water supply website to see what levels were in your water supply the last time it was checked. As if that isn't bad enough, tap water can also contain parasites that have survived the filtration and chemical treatment.

The most highly recommended solution I discovered was a full house water filtration system that cleans the water without the use of chemicals and then adds back the essential minerals such as calcium and magnesium. This, however, is highly expensive and certainly wasn't in my budget. I also didn't want to buy pre-filtered water because it came packaged in plastic bottles.

So, I spent a lot of time researching cheaper alternatives and finally found a simple solution called a 'charcoal water filter' that works for me. Simply put, this is a block of charcoal that I place in my glass water bottle. This removes impurities from tap water such as chlorine, raises the PH of the water to a healthier level and also adds minerals, such as magnesium, back into the water.

There are a range of different ones available online for less than £10 that last for six months.

Now, while I had found a solution for my drinking water, I still needed one for the water I cooked and cleaned with. After some more exploring I discovered ionic filters for taps and ionic showerheads. These are very low in price and easy to fit. The showerhead simply replaces your old showerhead and attaches to a standard shower hose and the tap filter just fits on the end of your household taps. These work by using a triple filter system, including Red Germanium, Grey Tourmaline and White Medical Stones that reduce the chlorine in the water. The added benefit is that my hair and skin are in much better condition now too, because the grey tourmaline beads create a negative ion process that helps your skin to better absorb nutrients and stay softer. Bonus!

Household Cleaning Products

I couldn't believe the number of different cleaning products I had in my home. I removed furniture polish, bleach, kitchen spray, bathroom spray, washing up liquid, antibacterial spray, floor cleaner and many more.

I now only use natural, organic, nontoxic products that I buy from my local farm shop. I have an all purpose cleaner that can be diluted and added to a spray bottle to clean everything around the home from mirrors and furniture to toilets and floors. This not only saves a lot of money but also means I no longer have multiple products taking up space in my home.

Recipe - For an even more natural alternative you can mix two parts baking soda with one part lemon juice and add boiled water to create a spray. This smells great and is very simple and safe to make.

Shower Gel

Our skin is our largest organ and absorbs whatever comes into contact with it so I wanted to ensure I was using something entirely natural to wash my body.

Recipe - I now make my own shower gel using simple ingredients. Simply melt half a cup of coconut oil over a low heat. Remove from the heat and add 20 drops of your favourite essential oils. Mix well and add one cup of castile soap (available online and in most health food stores). Allow it to cool completely before using a funnel to transfer it to a glass bottle. This shower gel smells great and lathers just like any normal product. The best part of this is you can create variations by using different essential oils each time you make it.

It also works great in the bath; simply add one capful under the running water.

Shampoo

While going through my chemotherapy I obviously wasn't in much need of shampoo. However, as soon as my hair started to grow back I began exploring natural alternatives. The best solution I have found is soap nuts. If you haven't heard of soap nuts don't panic, neither had I! It turns out they are small brown berry shells that naturally contains soap called saponin. This can be used to make soap and also to wash clothes (information on this later). They are available to buy easily online. Make sure you purchase organic ones; there is no point in going to the trouble of making your own shampoo if you are going to do it with soap nuts treated with chemicals.

Recipe - To make shampoo from soap nuts: simply place two cups of soap nuts in a large pan with six cups of water and simmer for fifteen minutes. Next, remove the pan from the heat and allow the mixture to cool completely. Drain the liquid through a sieve to remove the soap nuts and use a funnel to transfer it into a glass bottle. Finally, add some of your favourite essential oils to create a great smelling, natural shampoo. This recipe is adapted from the book 'Look Great Naturally' by Janey Lee Grace.

Soap Powder

My husband has eczema and sensitive skin and so, aside from my cancer, there were other reasons to explore a natural way to clean our clothes. I was excited to discover that you can add a handful of soap nuts tied inside a small fabric bag (or sock) directly to the washing drum. This worked great at first. However, after the first few months I felt like my clothes were no longer getting as clean as they did with conventional soap powder. I have since switched to using an 'ecoegg' and I am a complete convert. This small 'egg' contains two types of mineral pellets that produce powerful cleaning foam which effectively and naturally clean your clothes. The best part is that one egg costs less than £10 and can clean 720 washes of clothes. In case you are wondering, that is about three years worth of laundry in the average family home! So, not only is it natural and efficient, it is also hugely cost effective too. Best of all, they are dermatologically tested and great for people with sensitive skin, such as small children.

Moisturiser

Similarly to my shower gel and shampoo, I wanted to use a natural moisturiser. A friend recommended coconut oil and I started to do some research. I'd already started to use it for cooking with but I was far from convinced about its moisturising ability. I felt like I had gone a step too far when I began to consider rubbing myself with a cooking oil each morning. However, I was surprised to discover that there is loads of information available online listing all of the possible beauty uses of coconut oil. So, I thought I'd give it a go and I am a total convert. This stuff is actually amazing!

Coconut oil is solid at room temperature so to use it, simply take a lump from the jar and rub into your skin. It melts when it comes into contact with your body.

It is also an incredible make up remover and even removes waterproof mascara! It also makes a great face cream, even as a base for under makeup.

To use it on your face just take a lump of solid oil, rub it all over and wipe it off with a cotton wool pad.

I now always have three jars on the go: one for cooking; one I've added frankincense oil to for a body moisturiser; and one I use as a makeup remover.

Recipe - To add essential oils to coconut oil, let the sealed jar sit in a basin of hot water until this has melted and then add the appropriate amount of essential oil. I add about six drops of essential oil per 30ml of coconut oil. The combined oils will solidify again at room temperature and be ready for use.

Makeup

Binning all of my precious makeup was so hard for me. I love makeup and, let's be honest, cancer treatment doesn't make you look your best so, at the time, it had become an essential part of my daily routine. However, I didn't realise that a lot of makeup products contained parabens; reported for contributing to a number of detrimental health factors. This is especially relevant to women with oestrogen dependent cancers such as breast and ovarian cancer. So, in short, I needed to find natural makeup alternatives fast.

I am not one for recommending specific products so all I will say is please do your research when buying makeup and try to purchase natural, cruelty free products that are free from parabens and other chemicals. Now, more than ever before, it is increasingly easy to purchase natural makeup as more and more consumers are seeking alternatives that are cruelty and chemical free. As a result, makeup that is suitable will proudly be declaring these important values in their branding so you certainly won't have to read any small print.

I have been very pleased since switching my makeup range. Although it was expensive to replace all of it in one go, the products I bought all last longer than those that I had before. In fact, I wish I'd made the switch years ago.

Perfume & Deodorant

I don't use either perfume or deodorant now. After considerable reading, I decided these were just unnecessary, harmful chemicals being sprayed directly onto my skin.

Our bodies are designed to perspire, and our skin is

designed to release toxins so that they don't cause unnecessary harm to our vital organs. It seems completely unnatural then to try and prevent this process by stopping our bodies from sweating. Instead I now rely on the use of essential oils. Jojoba oil is particularly good as a deodorant. Simply rub a few neat drops into each armpit. I also use aromatherapy oil on my pressure points throughout the day. Lavender is great to help you relax and I love to use it before my daily yoga and meditation. Also, you will find that if you switch processed food for a plant-based diet, you will perspire less anyway and if you give up meat and dairy your sweat won't smell as strong either.

Dental Care

I stopped using fluoride toothpaste as soon as I was diagnosed instead choosing to switch to natural, organic toothpaste without foaming agents. This took a while to adjust to as it no longer had the same taste nor texture that I had been used to previously. However, I can now say with confidence that I prefer my new brand. I also switched my plastic toothbrush to a natural toothbrush made from bamboo. I, as you may be, was skeptical about whether this would have a detrimental effect on my teeth. After all, we are always told that we must use fluoride toothpaste in order to keep our teeth free from decay. However, since I have been diagnosed I have required less dental treatment than ever before in my life. This, of course, may also be attributed to my change of diet.

There is a lot of evidence about the toxicity of mercury fillings and, as such, cancer warriors often raise this as a concern for their health. Removal of these, however, can be more detrimental to a person's health than leaving them in situ as the patient may swallow some of the harmful by-products. There is a solution, however, that comes in the form of a biological dentist. These specialist dentists will fit a rubber mouth guard during the filling removal as well as an oxygen mask. This prevents any unnecessary exposure to the toxins within the mercury filling. This, unsurprisingly, doesn't come cheap and, at the time of writing, costs about £200 per tooth. With eight black fillings in my own mouth this is a huge financial commitment that I'm unable to make.

However, it still bothered me that I had these chemicals and heavy metals in my mouth and, potentially, in my blood stream and so, in the pursuit of ways of reducing my heavy metal exposure, I asked my own NHS dentist if he would be willing to fit a rubber mouth guard (albeit without the oxygen mask) while changing my fillings.

'Of course', came his unexpected reply. In fact, he went on to explain that when he has treatments himself, he asks his dentist to use one.

I was once again surprised at the wonderful responses that can come when we honour and respect our values and ourselves and speak up for our needs. I have since had some of my fillings replaced in this way and my exposure to chemicals and heavy metals has been significantly reduced at a much lower price tag.

House Plants

Did you know that house plants can absorb many of the toxins found in the average household and in exchange fill the surrounding air with wonderful fresh oxygen? The best plants for this are Spider Plants and Peace Lilies as they can both absorb a range of harmful toxins including formaldehyde and carbon monoxide. We now have one of these plants in every room within our home.

Clearing Space

I am not just talking about physically removing stuff, although that is very important, but also energetically clearing your personal space and home using a process called smudging.

If you've never heard of smudging it is the Native American practice of purifying a space with the smoke of sacred herbs, usually sage, to help clear negative energy from a room. Interestingly, this is also backed up by science, as burning herbs release negative ions that can boost your mood.

I smudge our home on a regular basis when working with my clients and also when conducting my daily shamanic rituals. Connecting with our home in this way has led me to become much more aware of not only the energy that is brought into it, but also the physical items. Off the back if this I have purged a lot of my belongings that were no longer of use, or which no longer brought me joy.

Getting rid of physical clutter and 'noise' is very cathartic and healing as it creates a more peaceful environment in which you can better focus on your holistic health and healing. There is something so refreshing and energising about the process of disposing of stuff that no longer serves you.

If this is a process that interests you then I highly recommend you read 'The Life Changing Magic of Tidying Up' by Marie Kondo. It really is life changing!

Top Tips - Making Your Environment Healthier

1. Replace candles with essential oils.

2. Try to avoid plastics wherever possible, switching to paper and glass alternatives if you can.

3. Drink filtered water.

4. Reduce your exposure to toxins by switching to natural house cleaning products, or make your own.

5. Switch to organic toiletries.

6. Declutter and clean your home.

7. Buy some houseplants.

8. Visit your dentist.

9. Clear out your makeup and invest in some more natural products.

10. Try making your own toiletries.

CHAPTER 12: BODY

Many of the aforementioned environmental and emotional factors influence the holistic manner in which our body heals and remains healthy. However, this chapter is focused specifically on what we put in and do with our bodies and covers a range of dietary changes as well as the importance of nurturing exercise.

Plant-Based Diet

While there is a lot of debate about the 'perfect anti-cancer diet', one thing that links all of the recommendations is the notion that you should increase the amount of plants that you consume on a daily basis. This is not to say that you should give up meat entirely, although this may be your preference. Instead, the 'plant-based diet' just suggests that the main aspect of each meal should consist of plants including fruit, vegetables, greens, pulses, beans and herbs.

Raw food is a huge part of my life now, due to the

belief that uncooked food has more nutrients in it than cooked food has. My breakfast is 100% raw, while my lunch and dinner is usually at around 50% raw. Not only does this save loads of time preparing food but it also allows you to introduce a lot more variety into your meals. I now love making new salads to serve with my cooked meals. Simply chopping up a couple of tomatoes, a small red onion, some coriander and then adding a squeeze of lime juice creates a super easy side dish that tastes amazing with curry. Similarly, fresh mango chopped up with a red chilli and a bunch of coriander is both delicious and refreshing.

Modern health recommendations have led us to believe that five portions of fruit and vegetables each day is optimal. However, in a plant-based diet this is considered a minimal requirement. People who want to get the majority of their nutrients from plants should be prepared to eat much more than this. Personally, I eat in excess of ten portions per day and always aim to have five portions during breakfast alone to ensure I have started my day well.

This may seem unachievable. I too wondered how on earth it's possible to eat that many plants in a day. However, as soon as you start replacing your other snacks with plants you will find that it is really simple. Now I love trying new varieties each week. For instance, did you know you can make a sugar free chocolate spread with black beans! Go on, have a search for recipes online. You will be amazed how simple it is to swap plants into your daily diet.

In the years prior to my diagnosis I used to have,

what I now recognise as, an unhealthy obsession with the amount of fat and calories I ate each day. I now realise that when following a plant-based diet and eating healthy food that not only do I no longer need to count calories but I also don't need to watch how much fat I eat either. You see, it isn't eating fat that makes you fat; it is eating sugar that makes you fat. I now only eat when I am hungry and could never tell you how many calories I've consumed. When you are eating real, un-processed food, you never need to worry about unhealthy obsessions with weight and calories ever again.

Minimal/No Meat

I tried, and failed to be a complete vegan. Despite having conducted extensive research into the meat industry and learnt the horrors of the hormones and chemicals that animals are exposed to before reaching our plate, I have been unable to give up meat completely. However, I now only eat fish.

Evidence shows that all non-organic meat is exposed to hormones as a way of ensuring that the animal develops more edible meat. For instance, chickens are given oestrogen to encourage them to develop larger breasts, as this is the part of the bird most in demand in the food industry. Now aside from the poor ethics and animal cruelty around the meat industry, my choice to give up meat was not based on this alone. Instead I recognise that, as I have a hormonal cancer, it is not in my best interest to expose myself to man-made hormones through what I eat. Of course I could have chosen to eat organic meat instead which has not been exposed to these hormones, however this is where the ethics came in. I am now a firm believer in not eating something that I could not kill for myself. This is why I still eat fish. I have caught and killed fish and, as a result, do not feel like a hypocrite when eating it. However, I think that modern society has created such a vast separation between the animals we see in a field and the plastic wrapped meat in a supermarket that people have become detached from the reality of what they are consuming. Now, don't get me wrong, I am not against farming and I fully appreciate that if we all became vegans that there would no longer be any animals in the fields. They are, after all, bred for the food industry.

Furthermore, aside from my ethical concerns, there is extensive evidence that our bodies are able to heal faster if we consumes less meat, instead favouring a plant-based diet.

One thing to note if you are a meat eater is what your meat was fed. Animals that are fed grass develop meat that is rich in omega 3 and very nutritious. However, animals that are fed on corn or grain develop meat that is rich in omega 6 that, while being needed in the human diet for optimal health, should not be over consumed as it can lead to many modern diseases. As a result, always try to source grass fed meat and note that even some organic meat is corn-fed, as it is cheaper than grass.

Green Smoothies (Not Juices)

So many people turn to juicing in a bid to promote

health and wellbeing. While I appreciate that this does carry many health benefits, and is certainly better than nothing at all, it is not my preferred choice. Instead I choose to make smoothies by keeping all of the ingredients whole. This not only creates a more filling meal, but it also maintains the fibre necessary for your body's optimal health and healthy digestion. Personally, I believe that juicing is a form of processing and thus creates a lesser alternative of the plant than nature had intended.

Recipe - Take a pear, three pieces of asparagus, a cupful of spinach, the juice of a lime, a handful of mint and half a cucumber with a cup of water and blend this together to create a super refreshing drink. This tastes as close to a mojito as I am ever going to get.

Please check out 'Green for Life' by Victoria Boutenko for further information and recipe ideas.

Ginger and Garlic

So many foods come with specific health benefits. However, I have chosen to select just two firm favourites: garlic and ginger. Both of these have incredible antibacterial and anti-inflammatory properties. Ovarian cancer, like many others, is an inflammatory disease and many patients are put on ibuprofen or other anti-inflammatory pharmaceuticals as a way of counteracting the inflammation in the body. I'm not a fan of over the counter medication and avoid it whenever possible so, instead I ensure garlic and ginger are in my diet daily.

Their antibacterial properties also make them great at helping to keep your body free from infection. As conventional cancer treatment often leaves a patient with a lowered immune system, these can be a great way of helping the body to avoid colds, viruses and infections. This is of specific importance to me as my splenectomy has left me with a permanently compromised immune system.

Ginger has the additional benefits of aiding digestion and helping relieve nausea, while garlic also regulates blood pressure and blood sugar levels. Both are really easy to include into meals, especially curries. Ginger is also a great addition to smoothies as well as snack balls.

Recipe - Blend two handfuls of nuts of your choice with a tablespoon each of melted coconut oil, raw cocoa, desiccated coconut, ginger, lime juice, plus a fresh chilli and three medjool dates in a food processor. Next, roll the mixture into bite sized balls to create some amazing sugar free snacks with a bit of spice.

Turmeric, Curry Powder and Other Spices

All of the many wonderful spices that are available for consumption today each have many health benefits and, as a result, I now have two cupboards full of organic spices that I use daily. While there isn't space here to go over them all I would like to share details of my two favourites: turmeric and curry powder.

Turmeric is the rootstalk of a tropical plant that belongs to the same family as ginger. One of the main components of the spice is a substance called curcumin that has long been debated for its potential healing benefits. In a lab environment this compound has demonstrated that when added to cancer cells they start to digest themselves within 24 hours. Now, while this is incredible, it is important to note that a lab environment and the body are entirely different. In a lab, the curcumin is added directly to the cancer cells, whereas when consumed, the curcumin has to go through the digestive system and many other processes before there is hope of it ever reaching the cancer cells. That said, I still consume it daily due to its many other health benefits including reducing bloating, improving digestive health and its antibacterial properties. You can also create a turmeric paste by adding a little bit of water and applying it to small wounds to aid healing.

Curry powder, which contains turmeric, also has many digestive health and antibacterial properties as well as showing evidence of boosting the immune system in the same way as garlic and ginger. As a result I use it daily when preparing our evening meals. In case you haven't realised already, we make a lot of curry in our house!

No Processed Food

So many foods are filled with preservatives and chemicals that the average layman can't even pronounce and yet are expected to consume without a second thought. No thank you! When I say no processed food I mean none. If it has ingredients then I'm not buying it or eating it. I make everything from scratch.

It was a slow, and sometimes messy, process but I have taught myself how to make so many things from scratch since my diagnosis. I have learned that I love cooking and exploring food and it has now become a great hobby for me. Am I the best cook? Definitely not. Is the food I make edible? Usually. Do I love to try new things? Absolutely!

Have fun in the kitchen and start exploring all the different things you can make from scratch. Not only will you save your body exposure to loads of preservatives, you will also save yourself money, as usually it is cheaper to make things yourself. Not only that but most shop bought, processed food is filled with sugar and salt that your body neither needs nor wants. Do yourself and your health a favour and slowly start learning how to make things from scratch. Before you know it, you won't miss the jars of sauces you used to buy because the food you make at home with real, fresh ingredients will taste much better.

Gluten and Dairy

I was diagnosed with a gluten allergy in 2010 and, as a result, I haven't eaten gluten since then. Personally I think gluten gets a lot of unnecessary bad press that has resulted in many fad diets that remove gluten. Eating wholegrain, unprocessed gluten should be separated from eating processed gluten. Highly processed, white bread or cakes are of course not as beneficial to your health as an organic, homemade, whole grain loaf. Replacing the former with a similarly processed gluten free alternative misses the point entirely. My advice? Unless you have a known gluten intolerance or allergy then, I think, there is no need to remove gluten from your diet. However, always make the conscious effort to eat unprocessed wheat and gluten rather than highly processed alternatives.

I gave up dairy for two reasons. Firstly, like meat, dairy is filled with artificial hormones that your body doesn't need. These can be damaging to your health, especially if you have a hormonal based illness. In fact, some studies have linked dairy products to the spread of some cancers.

Secondly, chemotherapy stripped my intestines of lactase, which is the natural substance found in a healthy gut and required to breakdown and process lactose. As a result, I have been left lactose intolerant. So even if I wanted to eat dairy I wouldn't be able to.

Personally (and I can't stress this enough) I believe that choosing to give up an entire food group is a very individual health choice that shouldn't be taken lightly. I don't think anyone should give up gluten or dairy because someone else says it is good for his or her health to do so. In fact, giving up either of them for a prolonged period of time can actually create intolerances within your body when you try to eat them again in the future.

I once had a personal trainer who told all of his clients to eat no gluten and to consume large amounts of dairy in the pursuit of a high protein, low fat diet. Having now done my own research, and since studied nutrition, I think this is a bullshit approach to health. Not only is it widely reported that excessive animal protein can cause cancer to grow and spread within the human body but also, despite what you might have heard, we do not need to consume excessive amounts of animal protein to build muscle. Neither do we need to exclude grains in order to achieve optimal health. So why do some personal trainers offer this advice? Simple. It creates fast, visible results. What they fail to mention is that these results are unsustainable long term and can have serious negative implications to your health. Instead, make lifelong healthy changes and you will achieve the same visible results while also improving your internal health.

Supplements

As with many aspects in the pursuit of the perfect 'anti-cancer protocol' there is a huge debate on supplements. You only need to spend a minute exploring online to see how many different recommendations there are around the many nutrients your body 'may' be deficient in. As with all of my advice, the key here is to trust your instinct. To believe that there is a one size fits all, magic supplement that will cure your cancer (or any other health condition) is unrealistic. This belief fails to recognise and honour that each of our bodies are biologically and physically different. Even identical twins have differences due to the varying experiences, foods and environments they have been exposed to.

If you really want to take supplements for your optimal health then you can seek blood tests to ascertain the exact levels of each known nutrient within your blood. This is not always freely available as part of a health care plan and you may have to pay extra for these tests, however it is always worth asking a member of your healthcare team.

Personally I have chosen very basic supplements. I take Vitamin C for my immune system. I take magnesium and calcium because my levels are regularly reported as low. I take Vitamin D3 because it is recognised in the literature that many cancer patients have a deficiency. I take Vitamin B12 for the same reason and because I don't eat meat which is the main source of B12 in our diets. I also take Vitamin K2 because it is reported for its anti-cancer properties and also because it works well with Vitamin D3. Finally I take Selenium and Zinc.

For a period of time I also took medicinal mushrooms - mainly reishi and chaga. This was following my cancer recurrence in early 2018, however I stopped taking them when I started having immunotherapy treatment. This was a requirement of my place on the trial and why I so strongly advocate that you tell your oncologist *everything* that you take. I sourced these mushrooms in capsule form through an integrated medicine doctor, Dr Kate James. In this way I could be sure that the doses were right for me as she was monitoring my blood levels to check for any contraindications. Medicinal mushrooms work in a similar way to immunotherapy by boosting your immune system and helping it to recognise and attack cancer cells. I had amazing results during the time I was taking them and remain a strong advocate for their use, however I do always recommend that they are bought from a professional who you are in regular contact with and not just from an online shop.

Once, final, piece of advice I will offer regarding supplements is to take organic ones. I don't see the point in spending my time and money sourcing organic food if I am then going to consume non-organic supplements. I always want to be putting the best into my body.

No Alcohol

I know this may be painful for many of my readers but I did give up caffeine and alcohol completely. In fact, the last alcoholic drink I ever had was 31st December 2015, eighteen days before my diagnosis and I have never touched a drop since. Now, while this wasn't hard for me as I've never been a big drinker, there have been times during my journey where a large glass of wine would have certainly helped to numb the reality. However, I want to keep my liver in tiptop condition and so I don't want to do anything to compromise its health.

At the very least, just reducing the amount of alcohol you consume can only have positive effects on your health.

No Sugar

Something of a controversy in the research I've conducted are the opposing views on sugar consumption following a cancer diagnosis. The literature all confirms that being overweight increases your likeliness of getting cancer but what if you were a healthy weight when you got diagnosed? Could limiting your sugar consumption aid your treatment and reduce your chance of a relapse?

Well, the answers aren't that straightforward.

The books I've read all agree that limiting sugar consumption should be a lifelong commitment following a cancer diagnosis. In particular 'Radical Remissions' by Dr Kelly Turner and 'Anti-Cancer' by Dr David Servan-Schreiber both talk about this at length, as do many academic articles. However, many cancer charities state that there is not enough evidence to support the need to limit sugar consumption and that during treatment cancer patients should eat whatever they want to maintain their strength and weight.

However when cancer patients are given a PET scan they are injected with glucose based radioactive dye because it goes to the cancer cells first, thus highlighting them on the scan results. This is because, while all cells require glucose, cancerous cells 'feed' on glucose faster than 'normal' cells.

So therein lies the controversy. On the one hand we are told that sugar is of no harm to someone with cancer and, often, patients can be encouraged to eat it in order to gain or maintain weight. On the other hand, however, research shows that cancerous cells will feed on sugar faster than other cells.

So what's my conclusion?

I know that while recovering from surgery, when I ate sugar I felt more pain in the following hours than I did on a normal basis.

I know I craved sugar on a ridiculous level in the

months before my diagnosis – we are talking a couple of bars of chocolate, a can of fizzy juice, a huge bag of sweets and several large spoonfuls of chocolate spread each day! This is a common factor in most cancer stories, with people often reporting similar abnormal sugar cravings prior to their diagnosis.

Finally I know that my CA125 levels reduced the most rapidly during the chemotherapy cycles when I consumed the least sugar.

So, whether it's a placebo effect or not, I still made the decision to cease all sugar consumption and I tell you what - I feel awesome for it!

'But what about 'natural' sugars?' you may be wondering. Well, firstly, let's get one thing straight, all food we consume is turned into glucose for our cells. When I say I've cut out sugar I'm talking refined, processed sugar and 'white' foods.

I still consume fruit. Yes it contains fructose but it is in a form that my body has to work to convert it. Also the nutrients it provides are essential to maintaining a healthy immune system.

I naively thought dark chocolate was a 'safe' option but many of the packs I've looked at contain at least 25g of sugar per 100g. That means they are made up of a quarter of sugar! Just picture that! I even found one that was 42g of sugar! Instead I now use raw cacao chips that are 100% sugar and dairy free and taste great. I like them over sliced pear with some grated ginger. Amazing!

Cutting out refined sugar is hard. It's one of the most addictive substances we consume. However, the less of it you eat, the less of it you crave. Also your taste buds change and you start to find that other natural food tastes much sweeter than before.

Of course, all of this could be nonsense in terms of helping my body to heal from cancer. I could stand just as good a chance while eating cake every day. I just don't know.

What I do know is that I have come through my chemotherapy reasonably well compared to some other people. My cancer markers are down. I haven't taken painkillers for over two years. I was diagnosed with Stage four B cancer and yet just seven months later I was told I was in remission and today, despite a cancer recurrence, I'm still very well!

All that really matters is that you eat what feels right for you and your treatment plan.

Organic

While I'm not going to be one of those people who preach that everyone should be vegan, I do preach that people should eat with a responsibility for the source of their food and the treatment of the animals and farmers.

I only eat organic food. This is not just to avoid the toxic chemicals, antibiotics, hormones, pesticides (and so on) added to non organic food and the soil it grows in, but also because it makes it easier to trace the source of my food and, in doing so, allows me to take responsibility for its impact on the environment.

Similarly I only eat whole foods and make everything from fresh ingredients so that I know, without any doubt, the source of everything I eat.

I could probably write a book on the research I have done into food alone since I was diagnosed, as it is an area I am extremely passionate about. However I won't go on and on (too much). What I will say, however, is that I know organic is more expensive and yes our household food bill has risen. However, I feel this is a small price to pay for health.

For me it's been about priorities and I prioritise knowing exactly what is in the food I eat. We live in a society where we find it acceptable to spend £3 on a takeaway coffee but won't pay £2 for organic eggs. Seriously! We need to get our priorities straight.
It is my firm belief that the food we eat defines our health.

If the cost of eating only organic food isn't possible for you then have a look online at the 'clean fifteen and dirty dozen' which will provide you with details of the food that is the most important to source organically (the dirty dozen), as well as those that absorb the fewest pesticides (the clean fifteen). This will enable you to make informed choices about your food.

I have provided a brief overview here to get you started.

The Dirty Dozen

In order of those which absorb the most toxins from the surrounding environment:-

- Apples
- Celery
- Sweet bell peppers
- Peaches
- Strawberries
- Nectarines
- Grapes
- Spinach
- Lettuce
- Cucumbers
- Blueberries
- Potatoes

The Clean 15

In order of those which absorb the fewest toxins from the surrounding environment:-

- Onions
- Sweetcorn
- Pineapples
- Avocados
- Cabbages
- Peas
- Asparagus
- Mangos
- Aubergines
- Kiwis

- Melons
- Sweet potatoes
- Grapefruit
- Watermelons
- Mushrooms

Physical Exercise

Moving your body is the simplest step you can take to improving your holistic health. Not only does it help your respiratory and cardiovascular health but it also helps you to maintain a healthy weight. Perhaps more importantly, however, exercise also moves the lymphatic fluid around your body more easily as well as helping to improve your digestive health. All of this combined shows that we need daily exercise in order to remove toxins from our bodies.

Regular exercise also helps us to maintain a state of calm and improves our sleep, both of which are especially important when trying to return our bodies to a state of ease. If that wasn't enough, it also helps regulate our blood pressure and resting pulse. Extensive evidence shows that people going through cancer treatment who exercise regularly respond better to treatment with fewer issues and demonstrate longer periods of remission.

You don't have to do anything overly energetic. Even just a daily walk will work wonders on your health. Find an activity that you enjoy and do it every day.

Detox

There are extensive examples of detoxes online ranging from liver cleanses to fasting. I am neither for nor against any of them and so I won't delve into them here. Instead I would like to offer a few very simple things you can do in your own home to help your body detox, aside from drinking plenty of water of course.

The first is to have a cup of warm water with a slice of lemon in it each morning. This is thought to help cleanse your liver and skin and, if nothing else, it is simple, cheap and tasty.

The second is to have regular salt baths. My personal preference is Himalayan Salt. Add a cupfull of salt to a hot bath and soak for about 20-30 minutes. It's important to have a shower afterwards to rinse your body of any toxins that may have come to the surface. Also, it is important to drink lots of water afterwards to help keep your body hydrated.

In addition to this I also have regular hot stone massages. These are a great way for not only easing tension out of my body, but also for helping to breakdown and release toxins. Due to the location of my cancer, and my surgery, the masseuse has to adapt the massage to meet my individual needs. For this reason, if you have cancer too, it is essential that you check with your oncologist to see if a massage is a safe option for you.

I also use a 'blanket' infrared sauna. These nifty devices cost around £200-250 and work like a normal infrared sauna. Instead of purchasing and installing a large sauna, which you may not have the space or money for, with these you can lie on your floor or bed wrapped up and meditating while receiving the same benefits of sitting in a giant sauna.

There is so much research about the therapeutic benefits of infrared saunas. They are great for detoxification, boosting immunity, helping reduce fatigue, aiding relaxation and helping with aches and pains. Needless to say they are shown to treat a number of symptomatic affects associated with cancer. I wouldn't be without mine now.

Practice Deep Breathing

Since my diagnosis I have developed a deep respect for the sadly underrated holistic health benefits of deep breathing. Through breath awareness it is possible to gradually bring breathing under greater conscious control and, through this, open up physical and psychological changes. Through learning how to breathe deeply and effectively, it is possible to create a link between the body and mind and, as such, through breath control we can control the emotional and physical state of our body.

Prolonged ineffective breathing patterns, such as isolated chest breathing can result in parts of the body being left with an insufficient supply of oxygen. This can lead to disease, as the cells and tissue are unable to function properly. It is only through the additional use of diaphragmatic breathing (or 'belly breathing') that the air breathed in is able to properly oxygenate the body.

'Belly breathing' not only improves the amount of oxygen in our bodies and, subsequently, our cells, but it also moves the abdominal organs with each breath. On inhalation, the organs are pushed outwards against the abdominal wall. On exhalation, the organs can return to their original position. Each breath therefore 'massages' the internal organs and thus stimulates blood supply, oxygenation and circulation. This can help to speed up the digestion process and activate the cleaning of the body and internal organs.

This deep breathing also creates a sense of calm and relaxation. This provides control over undesired emotional response patterns such as anxiety and stress. Thoracic (chest) and/or clavicular breathing, on the other hand, can actually *induce* the 'fight or flight' response and cause unwanted emotional responses. Indeed, anxiety, depression and confusion are all heightened in people with ineffective breathing patterns.

You may have noticed for yourself that when you are anxious your breath quickens and your chest rises and falls more quickly. By simply working on your belly breathing you will not only improve the oxygen and blood supply in your body, you will also help to maintain a state of calm and relaxation even in otherwise traumatic or emotionally challenging situations.

The easiest way to learn this health promoting style of breathing is to put your hands on your tummy and make your tummy big when you breath in and small when you breath out. You also want to breath out for roughly double the amount of time you breath in for. Try breathing in for a count of two and out for a count of four to begin with.

I practice my belly breathing daily and feel incredible for it. In fact, I would even boldly say it is one of the most important steps I've taken to improve my physical and emotional health since diagnosis. It's also one of the simplest!

Top Tips - Making Your Body Healthier

1. Eat more fruit and vegetables.

2. Cut down or eliminate the amount of meat in your diet.

3. Experiment with immune building ginger, garlic and spices.

4. Explore the use of supplements to support your diet.

5. Cut down or eliminate the amount of alcohol in your diet.

6. Buy organic food whenever possible.

7. Cut down or eliminate the sugar in your diet.

8. Move your body.

9. Explore ways of detoxing your body.

10. Set aside some time each day to practice deep breathing.

CHAPTER 13: SPIRIT

I'm not a religious person, although I greatly respect those who are. Instead I believe in universal energy, in doing good and in appreciating the gifts that nature brings us each and every day - the air we breathe, the food we eat, the water we drink and the shelter we can often take for granted.

For me, spiritual health is not about religion. It is about finding a state of peace and comfort within ourselves. While closely linked to our emotional health, I believe it goes beyond this, requiring us to find our purpose in life and embrace how we can be of service to the planet and universe as a whole.

Ultimately it is about uncovering who we, as individuals, can connect with and help others. Creating optimal spiritual health is, therefore about accepting who we are and our circumstances with a state of peace and gratitude and using this to make the world a better place, even if in a small way.

It is through development of my own spiritual health that I have been able to uncover the 'gifts of cancer' that I share with you in the next part of this book and why I give thanks each day for my wonderful life and the many challenges I have faced and, more importantly, overcome. Without these experiences I wouldn't be the person I am today and you wouldn't be reading this book!

Practice Gratitude

I remember the first time I prayed. It wasn't to God. I mean, I can't say I've ever been a great believer in an Almighty Being. In fact, to this day I find it hard to articulate to whom I was actually praying to but, needless to say, I still did.

It wasn't an overly spiritual moment. I wasn't kneeling beside a bed as we so often see in the movies. I wasn't in a church or a religious setting. I wasn't even in nature. No, I was lying naked in the bath.

I'd just had my first chemotherapy session the day before and with it had come the realisation that until this point, despite the many challenges life had thrown me, I had never experienced real pain or suffering. There I was lying bare to the world, stripped not just of my clothes but of all humility in my life. Since waking I had soiled my clothes, I had thrown up repeatedly, I ached to my core with the kind of pain that brings you to your knees, begging for death.

I was alone in the bath, sobbing to myself as I received the comfort of the warm water that surrounded me and all I felt was gratitude. I was not sad at the suffering I felt. Instead I felt unbelievable gratitude that the water that covered my body was offering me relief.

I'd had countless baths before and never had I appreciated them. That day however I was brought to tears by an overwhelming sense of appreciation for my life.

I did not pray to ask for healing. I did not ask for my suffering to be taken away from me. No. Instead I gave thanks to the universe for the relief. I gave thanks for the lessons that I was receiving and for the air that I was breathing.

From that day forward I did the same every single morning. I thanked the universe for the ability to make it to the bathroom, for the water that soothed me and for another day to live my life.

In those moments, each day, I made a promise to the universe. I promised that for as long as I was able to live that I would help others to receive the gifts of their adversities and to embrace their lives and all of its beautiful challenges with love and gratitude.

It's not been easy. There came times where I would have gladly given up in a heartbeat, but that sense of gratitude never left me. I knew that all over the world, in that very moment, there were people in worse situations than me who were praying to be in mine. I realised that however bad the moment may seem that it would pass and with it I would find moments of joy again. My unwavering gratitude for the moment I am living in has offered me the strength and hope to keep going on my journey.

However bad the moment may seem, I promise you that there is always something to be grateful for, even if it is just taking a moment to appreciate the fact that you are still breathing.

Yoga

Without doubt I owe my spiritual health, and indeed my holistic health, to yoga.

I used to think I had a fair understanding of yoga and what it could do for me. I now know I was wrong. Like many others, I had used yoga as a form of fitness and stress relief for several years to help me to cope with the high demands of my career. Following my diagnosis, I started to explore the deeper aspects of everything in my life and felt increasingly drawn to exploring my existing spiritual awareness and the 'inner knowing' that had led me to know I had cancer, despite being shunned away by medical professionals for many months prior to my diagnosis.

This growing interest in my spiritual health and the essential role it plays in achieving optimal emotional and physical health, led me to return to yoga following my surgery as a way to help me heal holistically and not just physically. With new insight I was ready to explore what yoga and meditation could teach me as I sought ways to heal all aspects of my life.

However, no one could tell me if it was safe. I'd been told I shouldn't expect to even walk up stairs for a few months, but here I was three months later, walking two or three miles daily and desperate to bring yoga postures back into my life. A deep inner knowing was telling me this was what my body needed and I wasn't prepared to give up.

Finally, admitting that no yoga studio was going to touch me, I approached a teacher training school. If no one knew if it was safe to teach me then I would learn how to teach for myself. I would become an expert in my own body and healing. Amazingly they took the risk and, just four months after my surgery, I enrolled in their 12-month training program.

Within the first few months something incredible started to happen. No longer was I just being taught about yoga as a form of fitness - the prevalent view in modern Western society - but, instead, I was learning about the holistic benefits of yoga. I was learning about pranayama (breath), chakras and a plant-based diet. This took me on a journey of self-discovery and healing as I began to change physically, emotionally and spiritually. I knew this was the healing journey I had craved.

I began to listen to my body, and not my medical team, about what I was now able to achieve. Having been told that I would be struggling to even bend to pick something up six months after my operation, I instead found myself training to be a yoga instructor, feeling physically, emotionally and spiritually more whole and more at peace with myself and my life than ever before.

I continue to baffle medical professionals at how well I am and I strongly believe that yoga and meditation have played a massive role in achieving this optimal level of health.

When I read the extensive literature on yoga I feel empowered by what I can achieve in life and have a firm belief that, with practice and guidance, the spirit can heal the body.

This is a notion that I would have shied away from in the past. I would have been curious about the possibility ,but wouldn't have let myself believe. Yet here I am, living proof of the possibility that yoga can offer us something more. This is something that I became so excited about sharing with the world, that it led me to launch my own yoga business through which I now regularly teach classes and one-to-one sessions, as well as hosting annual retreats - not something you typically expect from someone diagnosed with terminal cancer.

However, the benefits are not just physical. Despite common misconception, yoga is not just an additional aerobic exercise to add to the list of many fitness 'trends'. Although yoga will strengthen your body, by choosing to view it purely through a fitness lens, you will miss out on the fundamental aspects of yoga - the growth of your mind and of your spirit.

If people embrace yoga for all that it has to offer - unity of their mind, body, heart and spirit - then they will achieve holistic health and all the positives that it can ultimately bring into their lives. This is essential, now more than ever before, as we face universal challenges catalysed by negative emotions such as frustration, shame, grief, loneliness and anger - that can be resolved only through unity and improved relationships with those round us, with the world and, most essentially, with ourselves.

'Why then, does yoga involve physical postures?' you may be wondering. Well, without physical health, we cannot develop the mind or spirit to the same extent. For instance, when your physical state is compromised by sickness your mental state becomes clouded and unfocused. Yoga acknowledges the connection between mind, body and spirit and utilises this through postures, breathing and meditation to alter the physical capabilities of the body and, with them, the mind.

Through the use of postures, people who practice yoga are encouraged to become more aware of their physical movements and the role of their breath in these movements. By stilling their focus in this way they naturally become more focused on their mind as a result. Similarly, by gaining increased control over your mind, it is possible to move away from negative or self-destructing habits that often lead to mental anxieties and a state of dis-ease. This is because a still and calm mind allows health energies to accumulate that will ultimately only lead to improved physical health. In addition the tension we hold in our bodies is caused by stress and other negative emotions and life habits and if ignored will, over time, lead to Western health issues such as obesity, heart disease and even cancer. However, with gentle movement through yoga postures and a focus on the breath it is possible to learn to let go and undo the tension and stresses held within our physical form.

So, in order to focus on the physical movements of yoga, we must first focus on the breath and, in doing so, with practice, we will achieve a meditative state as we learn to still our minds. This improved relationship between mind, body and spirit ultimately leads to holistic health. This ability to control and still your mind and create a meditative state through movement and breath is what defines yoga as a 'state of mind', rather than an aerobic exercise.

Through my own daily yoga practice, I now feel a deep connection and passion for the spiritual benefits of yoga and the impact that these can have on every aspect of your life. The more I read about and practice yoga and meditation the more I strive to build a more compassionate and kinder world. This has led to me handing out random acts of kindness (more on this later) in a bid to improve the world in which we live. I do this in the hope that it sparks ripple effects of compassion.

Yoga has taught me the importance of having a warm and open heart and of treating all living things with love. This has brought me great peace, not only during my practice but also in my day-to-day life, even in the face of adversity, pain or uncertainty.

I now embrace a happy and fulfilling life flowing with joy and positivity. Having started my teacher training as a means of supporting my own healing I now want to share this knowledge with others and help them on a journey to recovery too, and not just those who have cancer, but all those living with dis-ease in their lives. Most importantly I want to encourage those I teach to embrace yoga as a way of life, rather than an aerobic exercise.

Meditation

Meditation has played a fundamental part in my life for many years, however its significance has understandably increased since my diagnosis. It is an extremely powerful tool in helping us to stay within the present and live joy-filled lives. I am often asked how I coped so well with adversity and my response is always the same: breath work, yoga and meditation.

With meditation we place ourselves in the here and now. We are no longer concerned with the past and no longer worried about the future. Now is the only reality we have.

Through regular practice we are able to turn our attention inwards and listen to our body, mind and spirit, evaluating whether or not they are in optimal health. Regular reflection in this way enables us to become in tune with ourselves and to be our own teachers when on the path to self-growth. It enables us to get to know ourselves and, in doing so, pushes us to develop through the wisdom and teachings of our experiences and circumstances.

By becoming more connected with ourselves and our thoughts and more open to turning our attention inwards, we are able to take this guidance and use it in a way that suits us. We are each different and, although we may find ourselves on the same path as one another, our learning will be different as each of our spirits seek to learn different things. Meditation helps us to tune in and listen to this so that we become experts in ourselves and our own needs. Perhaps if everyone were to focus on the preset moment we would live in a much more peaceful and content world.

It can be hard to know where to start with meditation if you have never tried it before. However, once you get into a habit of adding even just a few minutes of meditation into your life each day you will soon feel the benefits.

There are now loads of apps to help guide you through meditation and many cancer centers offer meditation courses for people with cancer and those who support them. These are amazing and I can't recommend them highly enough.

If you want to give it a go for yourself then simply find a quiet place where you won't be disturbed for a few minutes (easier said than done I know). Sit in a chair or on the floor. You want to be comfortable but still able to concentrate (rather than fall asleep). Next close your eyes and begin to focus on your breathing. It can help to place your hands on your tummy. Count your inhale for two and your exhale for four. Thoughts will enter your mind and that's normal. Just let them go without getting drawn into them. Meditation isn't about having no thoughts; rather it is about learning to let them go. After some practice you will no longer need to count your breath and, instead, will just be comfortable sitting quietly in a state of calm.

Doing this for a few minutes each day is not only

great for your mental and spiritual health but Dr Kelly Turner reports in her book 'Radical Remissions' that regular meditation has been proven to promote physical health in people with cancer, even late stage cancer. So it's definitely worth a try. As with the aforementioned deep breathing, it is sometimes the simplest acts that can improve our holistic health most drastically.

Energy and Touch Therapies

There are a number of different energy healing practices that can be useful in establishing and maintaining optimal emotional and physical health. While they are each very different from one another, I have grouped them together because I feel that it is a very personal choice when deciding which one resonates with an individual person.

Personally I have tried Reiki, Bodytalk, Crystal Therapy, Emotional Freedom Therapy (aka Tapping), NLP, Body Stress Release, Shamanism, Reflexology and Acupuncture and found all to be of use to me for different reasons. Rather than write about them all in detail here I invite you to use your inner guidance to explore them further.

I have trained in Reiki and Crystal Therapy since my diagnosis and, at the time of writing this, I am now also training to become a shamanic practitioner. That said, my two favourite touch therapies are Body Stress Release and Acupuncture.

There are also a number of other energy and touch

therapies that I haven't tried that you may wish to engage with as part of your journey.

Personally I think that anything that reconnects you with your sense of self and helps you to relax is of great benefit to your holistic health. Whether you believe in the treatment or not doesn't really matter. What does matter is that you feel supported and listened to by the practitioner and that you feel better afterwards. In fact, research shows that this is fundamentally more important than the actual therapy you choose.

As with any aspect of your treatment plan it is essential that you trust your instinct and try only those therapies that feel right for you. Also, be careful not to overload your body with loads of different therapies. Instead limit it to a maximum of one or two per week (or less) so that your body can integrate the work and truly benefit.

Believe in the Possibility of Healing

Of course, the most important thing you can do for your spiritual health is to stop focusing on the negative and start believing in yourself and the possibility of healing. You have the healing power within!

I believe that the most fundamental part of any healing plan is to maintain hope even when it seems completely unrealistic. I have had moments where I stared death straight in the eye, where I could have chosen to succumb and surrender my precious life. During those dark moments the only thing that kept me going was hope; hope that things would get better; hope that there was light at the end of the tunnel; hope that I would heal. I know that one day I won't survive one of these moments, but until that moment hope is serving to keep me alive and deeply loving every second of my life. I encourage you to always have hope and to believe in yourself and the possibility of healing no matter what.

A series of unusual life events made it easier for me to have unwavering hope and to believe in the possibility of healing. Right from the start, the circumstances of my life didn't have the most normal of beginnings. Just days after my conception my mum had elective surgery to be sterilised. Imagine her surprise then when a few months later, after being told that her pregnancy symptoms were 'her imagination', she discovered that yes, in fact she was pregnant and would soon be delivering her third child.

Rather than this leading me to develop a complex that my parents didn't want me, knowledge of these circumstances led me to always have a positive outlook and a deep inner knowing that, as cliché as it may sound, 'everything happens for a reason'. This, of course, was helped by my parents constantly reminding me that I was 'meant to be'.

As a result I perhaps had a different approach to obstacles than most people. I have never been easily defeated and, in reality, I love a challenge, and particularly those that are statistically improbable. At our wedding my husband stated in his speech that 'I've learnt when Fi says she is going to do something, however unlikely it may seem, it is best to just stand back and let her get on with it.' He's a smart man.

All joking aside, this wasn't the only time I 'cheated death'. In fact there were a number of unique occasions prior to my diagnosis; the time I was hit by a car; the time I had toxic shock; the time my heart stopped on an operating table. On reflection, I now like to believe that life was trying to get me to pay attention; trying to wake me up to the fact that I wasn't truly living.

When I was just four years old my mum walked into our living room to find me watching open-heart surgery on the TV. She'd left me watching cartoons while she went to get something in the kitchen, yet in the few moments that had passed I had changed the channel. She was horrified! That is until she realised my fascination. I wasn't scared. I was curious and I had a million questions to ask her. And so began my morbid curiosity with life and death and, most likely, my dark sense of humour - although perhaps I just got that from my Dad.

From that point, the line between life and death never frightened me. Instead, it fascinated me. The mechanics of our bodies working away under our skin stuck with me and I had a strong desire to become a medical doctor. Life, however took me in a different direction.

At school I was torn between a deep love of words and numbers and the creativity of making something with my hands. I loved English and Mathematics but Technological Studies and Art and Design made my heart sing. I was a persistent talker in class, always bored and, much to my teachers' annoyance, always distracting others. Yes I was 'that' pupil. However, despite spending most of my school career standing in the corridor or writing lines, I passed my exams with mostly As and Bs and had a choice of which University subjects I could pursue. By some miracle I found a course that combined both my passions and began studying a BSc Hons in Product Design - a course that had a strong basis of practical engineering.

On one otherwise insignificant day, just weeks before graduation, I was working on an electric disk sander in the workshop when an accident lead to both my hands being sucked in.

I don't remember the specifics of the incident. My first recollection is standing next to the sander, my hands cupped in front of me and covered with blood. Apparently I'd screamed so loudly the technicians had heard it in their soundproof booth. The first aider on duty, having only just trained, guided me to the sink and unravelled my fingers as he reassured me that everything was alright. 'Jesus Christ' came his instinctive, horrified response to the mess of bone and mangled tissue before his eyes as he quickly recomposed himself and began reassuring me again.

I was taken to hospital where the damage soon became clear. I had removed the finger pads off of all of my fingers on both hands. I would need skin grafts and there was a high likelihood that I would lose the fingers on my left hand. Surgery would take place the next day.

They performed the surgery while I was awake. I had a surgeon working on each hand as I lay there staring at the ceiling. I was fascinated to note that as they worked they talked to each other about going on a date. They were oblivious to my presence. Not once did they speak to me despite the fact I was awake. It was an eye-opening realisation that, in that moment, I wasn't a person to them. They were just doing their job. It was recollection of this fact that would guide me to later work in a career driven by the aim of ensuring person-centred health care in Scotland.

The following weeks were torture. I could no longer drive, I was in constant pain and, much to my dismay, I was now completely reliant on the help of others.

I attended regular check-ups during which the bandages were changed and the state of my healing was monitored. At one particular appointment I was informed that it didn't look like the skin grafts were taking hold on my left hand.

'You need to prepare yourself for losing two fingers if they don't start healing soon' came the disconnected update of the consultant.

I was terrified. For the first time in my life I started to question my sense of self and worth. It is incredible to acknowledge, on reflection, the juvenile attachment I had placed on my physical ability.

However, not for the first time, and certainly not the last, something miraculous happened with my body. Just eight weeks following the incident, during a routine bandage change with my local practice nurse, she began to examine my hands more closely than usual.

'Come over to the sink, I want to check something.'

She placed my hands under the running tap and, as crazy as it sounds, the failed skin grafts washed away. In their wake were not the gaping wounds we had all feared but instead beautifully healed fingers. My body hadn't 'rejected the skin grafts'. It had healed itself beneath them.

We looked at each other in disbelief. I no longer needed any bandages. My hands were fine. Well, albeit minus any fingerprints but hey, let's not be picky!

This personal experience that healing is possible when you least expect it remained a guiding light for me following my cancer diagnosis. I wish more of us were led to believe in the healing capabilities of our bodies. This would provide hope rather than despair and a sense of helplessness. More importantly it would offer control, gifting us the power to take ownership of our health at whatever stage in our journey and regardless of our prognosis.

As you navigate your way through your own healing journey back to wholeness, I encourage you to believe that your body knows how to heal itself. Just as it heals a cold, a cut or a bruise, it can also heal greater dis-ease. All it needs are the right circumstances. Go inwards, connect with your intuition, take back control and help your body to heal.

Trust Your Instinct

Above all, the key to holistic health and, in particular spiritual health, is to trust your instincts and listen to your 'inner knowing'.

When on a healing journey following a cancer diagnosis (or any other dis-ease) you can quickly become overwhelmed by the amount of recommendations out there for improving your health. I've been there and I know it can be exhausting. However, what is most important is that you listen to what feels right for you. You know your body best.

I had a deep inner knowing that I had ovarian cancer. I didn't just know that something was wrong; I knew it was ovarian cancer. Despite specialists, tests and machines indicating otherwise for several months before I finally received the diagnosis that confirmed my fears, I had an unwavering faith that I knew exactly what was wrong with my body. It was the same inner knowing that had told me when I had an ectopic pregnancy; when my cancer had returned; and also many other things, of which there are too many to detail in one book!

I now use my inner knowing to guide me when I am making decisions about what is best for me in order to heal holistically. Sometimes people recommend things for me to try that, on paper, appear ideal for my diagnosis, however my instinct says no.

Similarly, sometimes I try stuff that isn't backed up by any scientific data. For example, from day one, I believed that time outdoors under moonlight was good for my holistic health. At the time I had no evidence to back this up but it just felt important to me. Now, training as a shaman, I know I was right to trust this guidance and 'moon bathing' and full moon rituals have become a regular part of my spiritual practice.

Ultimately the point I am trying to make is that the best thing you can do for your health is to listen to what feels right for you. Really listen. Only then can you have any hope of awakening your healing power within, improving your holistic health and starting your own journey back to wholeness.

Top Tips - Making Your Spirit Healthier

1. Start a gratitude journal and list what you are thankful for each day.

2. Try Yoga.

3. Meditate.

4. Try some energy and/or touch therapies that resonate with you.

5. Believe in the possibility of healing.

6. Have hope. Always.

7. Trust your instinct.

8. Spend time in moonlight.

9. Don't overload your body with different therapies. Instead chose one or two that you love and focus on them.

10. Set time aside just for you each day. Five minutes is better than nothing.

PART FIVE

CANCER IS MY GURU

CHAPTER 14: HAPPINESS

True happiness lies with understanding, acknowledging and accepting ourselves and our place within the world, regardless of our circumstances. It is the state of mind we achieve when we accept our reality, let go of what we thought would, or wanted to, happen and accept what has happened, or will happen.

This is how I approached my cancer diagnosis. It was an unexpected and life-changing event. It wasn't what I imagined or hoped for, but it became my reality. I had a choice to respond to it with bitterness and resentment, but in doing so I would have missed all of the gifts and lessons it had to offer. Instead, I embraced it as a blessing and let the opportunities it had brought wash over me and filter throughout my life. As a result I am now grateful for my cancer and the clarity it has brought me. I have a better quality of life and stronger relationships than I have ever had before. I am happier now than I have ever been in my life, having let go of who I thought

I was meant to be and instead embracing who I really am with love and acceptance.

Before my diagnosis I was not happy. I did not accept myself and instead I, like so many other people, judged myself constantly. I judged what I ate, how I looked, how I acted, what I wore, how I spent my time, how my home looked, you name it. I was completely self-loathing. Now I no longer judge myself but instead embrace my authentic self and strive to always act with kindness in my heart. If we approach life in this way then we can be content in the knowledge that the result will be the best that it can be. I've learnt that this is the key to living a happy life that is filled with joy.

Staying Positive

The question I get asked over and over again is 'how do you manage to stay so positive?'

Increasingly I believe it's because I choose to live. I don't let the words 'stage four', and everything they really mean, sink into my consciousness. I just live my life one day at a time and simply try to do my best in each moment.

Of course, I still have moments of realisation so debilitating I can't move. Moments of panic so strong I can't breathe. The thought of my life being over is never far away. The promise of tomorrow is never taken for granted. I am, after all, only human. However, I'm not sad or depressed. These moments don't remove my positivity but rather validate its importance.

I've come to realise that how I stay so positive shouldn't be the question. Instead the question should be about why I stay so positive.

The answer to that question is much more important. I stay positive because I know better than most how precious life is. I stay positive because I know how important it is that we never take a single moment for granted. I know how valuable each breath we take truly is. I stay positive because I realise that my life is a gift and I am filled with gratitude each and every day that I wake up.

Staying positive is easy once you start to feel gratitude for everything in your life. I encourage you to enjoy each moment and love with all of your heart because none of us are promised tomorrow. Make the day count. Make the day a day to be grateful for. Make the day good. Because life is too precious to waste.

Celebrate Today

Since cancer entered my life I have found myself approaching life with a deep connection, gratitude and positivity towards the world around me. Other people have often questioned this approach wondering how anyone could be grateful for a cancer diagnosis and in particular one so advanced. However, I believe that my approach is essential if I am to learn from adversity, to grow as a person and to maintain holistic health.

I used to think I'd want to celebrate the milestones of my journey; the anniversary of my diagnosis, the anniversary of my surgery, the anniversary of my remission and so on. I waited desperately for these days to arrive. At times, like after my surgery, I thought I'd never make each of these milestones. However, when the milestones came I felt no cause for celebration and I realised that these dates were no more special than any other day on my journey.

Cancer has taught me that every single day is a celebration, that each breath I take is more precious than the last. Each moment I get to spend with my family, each hug I receive from my sister's incredible children, each joke I share with my friends, each date I have with my wonderful husband; these are the real milestones. These are the tiny celebrations that add up to a life I never thought I would have the privilege of living.

You see, if you embrace the gifts that cancer brings - the knowledge that there is no tomorrow, the opportunity to embrace each and every beautiful minute we spend alive (yes even the seemingly crap ones) - then you don't need to celebrate a particular date because you are already celebrating each and every moment. You are already celebrating being alive and that's more important than any party to mark a specific milestone. Today is your milestone. The breath you just took, the pulse in your veins; these are what matter.

Don't wait for a special occasion or a significant date to celebrate being alive. Celebrate today! Laugh today! Love today! Above all, embrace everything in your life for the gift that it truly is!

Each day take a moment to be grateful for everything

and everyone in your life, including (perhaps especially) the challenges you face. Everything is an opportunity to learn and to grow and to become the best version of yourself. This is why I am so grateful for all that cancer taught me. I wouldn't have become the person I am today without it.

Take a moment each day to remind yourself of all the wonderful things that are happening despite (or even because of) the adversities in your life. Each and every moment is a gift to cherish.

Redefine Success

Society often tells us that success is having it all: the house, the partner, the car, the career, the holidays, the money and so on. The list is seemingly endless. But who made this list in the first place? Who decided that this is what success is? And, more importantly, what does it cost? Our relationships? Our joy? Our health?

Before I was diagnosed I was caught up in this societal view of success. It was what I strove for. It was what I spent each precious day in search of. From a young age I had watched my two older sisters as they studied and went on to receive qualifications and careers. I watched as they left the family home and bought their own property. I wanted that. I wanted the career, the house and the possessions.

So I studied. I got my Honours degree. But that wasn't enough. So I went back to University and I got my Ph.D. I worked day and night in dedication of completing it in the three years you are 'meant to'. As a result, I was awarded my doctorate just a few months after my 26th birthday, an endeavour that cost me the freedom of my 20s. Next I wanted the 'perfect' job. I took on several national research roles, each requiring hours of daily commuting and limited time with my husband. Feeling that I wasn't pushing myself hard enough I then began to fill my private life with ambitious tasks. I volunteered, trained for a marathon and studied hypnotherapy and psychotherapy. I filled each moment of down time with social activities with friends. It wasn't unusual for my hubby and me to have at least six events to attend every weekend. I never just sat. I never let myself be still. I was only happy when I felt like I was achieving something or working towards some invisible goal set by society. When the words 'stage four cancer' entered my life, however, everything changed in an instance.

The timing couldn't have been more ironic. I'd just landed my dream job. I was about to take on the role of 'User Research Lead' within the Scottish Government, working with an incredible team who, like me, were driven by a passion to make Scotland better. Life, however, had other plans. I was diagnosed on what would have been my first day and signed off work immediately. I never even made it through the front door.

I hadn't realised how much my sense of identity had been built around my career. I found the realisation that I wouldn't be working for the foreseeable future really hard to deal with at the time. I'd been so busy creating an outward facing persona of a happy, career-driven woman that I no longer had any idea who I was without it.

As my health started to improve, I had many conversations with my medical team about my return to work. These were always met with a look of concern: concern that I wouldn't manage the two hour commute; concern that I wouldn't manage the stress; concern that my brain function wasn't what it used to be; concern that my health would suffer; concern that I wasn't making the right choice.

I struggled with this. My fierce independence and stubbornness often led me to believe that I had to prove that I was still capable and that, one day, I'd be walking through the doors and starting my career as a civil servant.

As time passed, however, I started to appreciate these concerns and understand that I was no longer the same person who had applied for the role. During my absence from work I had begun to embrace getting to know who I really was and what mattered most to me. I began to realise that not only had the capacity of my body and mind completely changed but so had my spirit and, with it, my priorities.

I had a few more heartening and honest discussions and then I made a final decision to leave my long sought after job.

This was not an easy choice by any means. Not only was I leaving a career path I'd dedicated my life to but also, on a more practical level, my husband and I would be shifting to living on one wage. However, I refused to let my decision be swayed by status or money or what people would think. Instead I was overwhelmed by the realisation that, above all, I wanted to spend the rest of my life improving the lives of others in a way that would serve my soul and make my heart sing. For the first time in my life I was allowing my values to align with my sense of purpose and it was freeing me to follow my dreams. Guided by my instinct, I felt no worry or concern about the outcome. I just knew it would be all right so long as I was following and trusting my instinct.

This realisation was key in my decision to challenge the societal standard that suggests success means employment and status and money. Instead I prepared myself for the unknown (and possibly terrifying) path of un/self employment. And I have never regretted my decision. In fact it was the best decision I have ever made. Three months later, I launched my own business as a yoga instructor for adults and children. Despite my diagnosis and the associated risks of my health status changing at any time, I made the choice to follow my dreams. Unsurprisingly, I was terrified. What if no one came to my classes? What if I was making a huge mistake? What if people valued me differently?

I realised that despite all that cancer had taught me, I was falling into the old societal view of success. I was worried about what other people would think. I was worried about money. I was worried about status. The more I thought about it I began to notice that these were not my fears. They were, instead, the fears that society had placed on me. These fears are fed by a scarcity mentality and inflicted on us to ensure a consumer driven society.

So I took some time and re-evaluated the situation.

What if it was okay not to worry how busy or quiet my classes were? What if success was just running the classes, regardless of how many people came to them? What if it was introducing someone to yoga for the first time?

In that moment I made the decision that success would just be the act of launching my business, with the intention of helping others to embrace their own self-care and healing power within. I wouldn't measure my success on societal standards but instead on how I felt inside and how I made those I connected with feel.

The result was life changing. Overnight I was no longer stressed. It was that simple. I was finally doing what I had always dreamt of doing and it was as if the Universe was conspiring to support me. Everything fell into place, aligning with my new mindset, and I found I was able to effortlessly run my new business, despite have a serious medical illness.

Cancer taught me that success is not about money, status or power. It is about being true to your soul, your values and your purpose and having the courage to step forward on your path, even in the face of uncertainty. I don't know what my future has in store for me but I do know that wherever it takes me I will embrace it with all of my heart and spirit.

Recently, I turned to my husband and asked, 'Do you think I'd have spent today teaching children yoga if I hadn't got cancer?'

'No, I think you'd have spent the day stressed and have come home exhausted' came his honest response.

It made me think - I could have let cancer define me and ruin my world, but instead I chose to let it guide me to follow my dreams. I'd wanted to start up my own business working with children for as long as I can remember but I'd always put it off saying that the time wasn't right. I'd used a range of excuses to convince myself to set aside my dreams, ranging from money to status to time. Cancer, however, taught me that the timing is never right, it's up to you to make the timing right!

I only wish it hadn't taken getting so sick for me realise that success comes from within and that our careers don't define us; our values do.

What if success is just doing what we have always dreamed of? What if it is following our dreams with the best of intentions and kindness in our hearts and not getting caught up in the outcome? What if success is taking the leap of faith to follow your dreams? What if it's not taking the promotion but instead valuing your time over money? What if our success is no longer measured in money or status but instead by how happy we are?

If I can write a book, train as a yoga instructor, Reiki practitioner, crystal therapist and Shaman and set up my own business while going through treatment for stage four cancer then anything is possible. You can make the decision to follow your dreams now. Don't wait until the elusive 'tomorrow' when you have the money, the time, or something else. Do it today! Do what makes your heart sing and you will become unstoppable. I'm not saying that it will be easy or that there won't be challenges, but I promise you won't regret it.

CHAPTER 15: LOVE

I could tell you that my journey has been filled with screams and tears, with pain and suffering, with anger and fear. And of course there have been moments where these things have been present. However, in reality what has filled my journey most of all is love. Every day, every moment, every breath, has been touched by love.

Before cancer I would often worry that I wasn't loved. This may surprise some people as I'm told that I always come across as highly confident. However, on the inside, I always worried what others thought about me. I always worried that I wasn't enough. This, I'm sure, was a result of various life experiences including the abusive relationship I detailed previously. It took a cancer diagnosis for me to accept the love of those around me. From the moment I announced my diagnosis people began to express how much they loved my husband and me. No longer was their love left unspoken. Instead it was suddenly expressed in countless ways. Every day we received messages, cards and phone calls, each filled with love. However, I couldn't help but wonder why so many of us often don't tell people how we really feel until moments of tragedy.

Before my diagnosis I would have been shy about telling people I loved them but not now. Now I share my unfiltered love around like glitter. I don't want the people I love to ever have any doubts about how I feel about them.

Life is so precious and there are no guarantees about tomorrow so if you love someone, care about someone, value someone, admire someone then tell them today. Don't wait until one of you are sick. You never know how in need of your love they may be. Just imagine how happy we could all make people feel if we told them how loved and cherished they truly are.

Relationships

I am so blessed to have had so many wonderful people come into my life as a result of my diagnosis. I have made many new friendships with people who have had or have cancer. The support we can offer each other is priceless and without it I wouldn't be where I am today. Cancer has also brought old friends back into my life - rekindling friendships lost or forgotten but still full of love and happy memories. It has also strengthened many existing friendships. Each of these friendships fill me with love, hope and joy every day.

Sadly, however, cancer has also stripped me of some relationships; relationships that I had long believed were an integral part of my life. The pain of their end cut me deeply.

I thought long and hard about whether to write about this in my book, in particular in a chapter entitled 'Love'. However, while I try to focus on the positives in my life I also wish to be honest and open in the hope that my words will help others. Having discussed the topic of broken relationships with many other warriors I have discovered that, sadly, friendships falling away following a cancer diagnosis (in particular a late stage, incurable diagnosis) is frighteningly common. In fact most of the warriors I connected with expressed a personal experience of similar loss. Often this loss was of relationships that had spanned years, if not decades, of happy memories.

So, why is this the case?

Perhaps we lose some of our closest friends because it is more painful for them, than for others, to watch us go through our journey or for them to accept that they may have to witness our slow, and perhaps painful, demise. Or maybe it is because they can no longer identify with us as a person now that cancer, and the associated treatment, is changing our very sense of being. Perhaps, it is because they weren't real friendships in the first place. Possibly, now that we are no longer able to be the friend we once were, we are no longer of service to the person who played such a valued role in our life. Or, perhaps our diagnosis has changed us so much, we are no longer able to relate to one another.

In reality, the reason doesn't matter. The pain of a broken friendship still hurts the same, especially when you are coming to terms with your own mortality.

I have had so called friends express their annoyance that I no longer have the energy to spend time with them. Others have expressed their jealousy that I have made new 'cancer' friends. I've been called selfish for putting my health first and for leaving behind the lifestyle that once defined our relationships. I even had one tell me I was selfish for spending my time raising awareness for ovarian cancer and sharing my story online instead of spending time with her. These, I fear, were not real relationships in the first place and, perhaps, their removal from my life is another gift cancer has brought. I am still working through this.

In some cases friends came back into my life once my cancer was in remission and I started to resume a more active life again. Things worked at first but when my cancer returned they never wanted to discuss it. I felt I couldn't share my fears with them and instead, while supporting them in their life, I received no support for mine. This was no longer the type of relationship I was prepared to spend my precious time on. Sending them love and light always, I parted ways with them once again.

While I can't offer any solutions on how to mend a broken relationship following a cancer diagnosis, be reassured that it is not uncommon and, if this has been your own personal experience, you are certainly not alone. What I can assure you of is that you will more than likely meet and connect with many new wonderful people on your journey with whom you will develop rich and fabulous relationships.

For me, the greatest gift has been the people who have stood by me throughout my journey, and those that I have met whilst on it. These are the deepest friendships of all. They have been tested and through unwavering love, they have survived. Now that's the kind of people I want in my life.

Top Tips - The 'Friends' Cancer Will Introduce You To

What surprised me most when my cancer returned in December 2017 was the reaction from some of the people in my life. There was a definite lack of support that had been there when I first had cancer. Now, before I continue, I want to make it clear that I am not blaming anyone. I have cancer and I know that, even still, when my fellow warriors had a recurrence I had no idea how unbelievably awful they felt until I actually faced it for myself.

So, I am writing this firstly in recognition and admittance of this and secondly to help others know how to support a friend or loved one with cancer/after cancer/following a recurrence.

This section was written with the help of my Irish teal sister, Carol Bareham. Please read it with our dark senses of humour in mind.

1. The 'Gleeful/Gossip' Friend *'So, tell me all about your hospital appointment. How did it go? What did they say? You must be so scared. How do your family feel? It must be so sad for* *them. What about [insert partner's name]? It must be just awful for the two of you and your relationship.'*

You can tell this friend apart from all of your other friends because they have a slight smile on their face and they seem to emphasis every word they say with a slight undertone of glee. You know they don't actually give a shit about what happened in the hospital and that they are having this conversation so they can feedback to others. The biggest tell-tell-sign that you have encountered this friend is the use of the word 'must' instead of actually asking you. They are projecting their thoughts onto you and they are never positive ones. My response is usually 'why 'must' I/my family/Ewan feel that way?'

2. The 'Your Situation Reminds Me of When I went Through Something Completely Unrelated' Friend *'Oh you had a complete hysterectomy, I know exactly how you feel. When I had a c-section it was so painful I could barely pick up my baby.'*

Bleh! Just F off with yourself will you! I'm sure this needs no explanation but, just in case, firstly, a c-section in no way is anywhere near the same as open abdominal surgery to remove all of your reproductive organs and, secondly, they have a baby! How about they be grateful for that in front of the friend who can't have children. Enough said.

3. The 'My Friend Has Cancer, Pity Me' Friend *'I'm having a really hard day because my pal has cancer...'*

Now, of course, your friends are going to have really shitty days where the reality of your diagnosis hits them like a ton of metaphorical bricks. However the 'friend' I am referencing here is not the same, instead they are 'using' your situation for pity, rather than because they are genuinely upset.

4. The 'Let's Pretend it's Not Really Happening' Friend *'You look great, what you been up to?'*

You've just come out of hospital following a a week long admission. They know you've just come out of hospital. Yet, they cannot bring themselves to mention the fact. Instead they act as if nothing is wrong at all. However, you see the silent plea in their eyes and you hear the fake cheer in their voice. You know that this friend is probably hurting just as much as you and that mentioning cancer or hospital would result in them trembling in sadness. So, instead you find yourself responding with 'I'm great thanks, how are you?' What would probably be better for you both would be a good cry together.

5. The 'I Had This One Friend Who Survived Cancer' Friend *'I had a friend who had [insert a type of cancer completely unrelated to yours - in particular one that is much less aggressive or caught earlier than your own] and they were completely cured so you will be fine. You just have to stay positive and everything will work out just as it did for them.'*

This friend is not dissimilar to the aforementioned 'Let's Pretend it's Not Really Happening Friend'. They are clutching at anything that will make them believe that there is no possibility of losing you. I've learned to thank them politely and move on because I know they are hurting inside and that trying to educate them on my diagnosis will only cause them more pain.

6. The 'Whispering' Friend *'So, do you think your 'cancer' [insert hushed tone] is the reason you're not well again?'*

I used to want to scream 'are you a fucking idiot, of course I do, I have STAGE FOUR CANCER.' But I've learned that this is not the most helpful response. Instead I politely say, 'my symptoms are in keeping with a recurrence. Let's see what my scan results show.' My fellow warrior friend recently joked to me that 'cancer is the equivalent of the word Voldemort in Harry Potter: it can't be named.' This is a sad but true fact for some friends.

7. The 'Pity' Friend *'I feel so sad for you [insert head tilt].'*

Of course there is nothing wrong with a friend telling you they feel sad for you, but the pity head tilt makes me want to gag. I don't think anything makes my skin crawl more than someone pitying me. Worse still is the friend with fake pity - see 'The Gleeful/Gossip Friend' above.

8. The 'I've Had the Worst Day' Friend *'I've had such a bad day, I'm so tired and stressed...and so on and so on.'*

Picture this: you are in hospital, you've just had a dose of chemotherapy that is destroying all of your cells; you've vomited on yourself several times; you've literally shit yourself; you've lost all your hair; you are recovering from surgery; you have been told you might die; and so on...sometimes, just sometimes, your patience wears a little thin when people moan to you about stuff in their life that they have the power to change and/or fix.

9. The 'Really? Again?' Friend *'But, I thought your cancer had gone?'*

No matter how many times I've explained that my cancer is incurable so many people were shocked when it returned. The worst part of this friendship is that it is like they used all of their energy dealing with your cancer the first time round. You are often left feeling like your cancer is an inconvenience to them because you have it again - after all, how dare you be so selfish as to have cancer more than once! I struggle to have time for these people.

10. The 'Invisible' Friend '...'

This is the hardest friend to come to terms with because one day they are there and the next they aren't. Maybe they just fade away; maybe they stop messaging or calling; maybe they are always busy when you are trying to catch up with them; maybe they block you on social media; maybe you have a big fight. It doesn't matter which scenario causes you to no longer be in each other's lives, the pain is still the same.

Of course, there is a flip side to the coin. For every friend that doesn't know what to say or how to act there is the friend who holds you in their heart as they have always done. Here are just a few examples of some of the most precious encounters I've had since my initial diagnosis and recurrence.

1. The Friend Who Treats You Exactly The Same

You may have cancer but, guess what, you are still exactly the same person as you were yesterday and that you will be tomorrow. Friends that hear my concerns but don't let me wallow in self-pity, instead near slagging me off, are my favourite kind of people. Some of my favourite comments over the past two years are: 'Can I wear nipple tassels to your funeral?'; 'I'll just be delighted to not have to make gluten free, vegan shite anymore to be honest.'; 'Stop making it all about you all the time Fi'; 'Man, you always have to go one up don't you?'

And sometimes it's not just the cheeky comments that make all the difference. Sometimes it's the little actions that make you realise that your friends still see you as you. Here are just a few lovely examples: Friends that ask you out for spa days when you don't have hair and aren't feeling girly - they still see you as gorgeous and feminine. Friends that bring their new shoes to show you when you are in hospital - they are bringing some normality to their visit rather than talking about cancer all the time. Friends that pop in for a cuppa while you are having treatment - rather than making it weird and awkward, they treat it just as if you are meeting in a cafe.

The friend who brings their kids to see you in hospital - after all, why shouldn't you enjoy the company of children just because you are in the care of medics. The friend who brings you a takeaway - need I say more.

2. The Friend Who Sends You Pictures To Make You Smile

Sometimes friends don't know what to say, and that's ok. I mean, half the time I don't know what I want them to say anyway. The key is to say *something*. If you don't say anything then you become the aforementioned 'Invisible Friend', and no one wants that. Instead, I have many friends who simply send me a picture that will make me smile or who say 'I have no idea what to say' and then send me a picture. This is beautiful and perfect. It's true what they say, a picture really is worth a thousand words.

3. The Friend Who Listens

Usually I just want to talk about normal, funny, everyday stuff. However, sometimes I want to talk about the hard reality of my health situation. During these times it's really good to have a friend who can, just for a moment, set aside their own concerns and questions and listen to what I have to say. I know it's painful for them and I certainly don't want our precious encounters to be overrun by 'cancer chat' but it is nice to know that I have friends I can vent to when I need to. It's also nice to have friends I can cry with too.

4. The Friend Who Has Cancer Too

On the darkest days and at your lowest points, there is no one who can pick you up as quickly as someone who has cancer too, in particular, someone with the same diagnosis as yours. Sometimes just having a brief conversation, laugh or bitching session with someone who just 'gets it' is all the therapy you need to pull yourself back together and face the world again. For this reason, I strongly recommend you connect with people in a similar situation to your own.

Find Love in Unexpected Places

You may expect an oncology ward to be a sad place; a place of suffering and tears; of pain and death; a place where people have lost hope and with it their spirit or vibrancy taken by the many drugs, treatments and procedures.

You'd be wrong.

I remember at the start of the film 'Love Actually', Hugh Grant describes the love you often see in an airport; people greeting one another with hugs and kisses and happy stories of fun and laughter. I liken this to my experience of an oncology ward.

You see in an oncology ward there are no arguments, no stress, and no hatred. There is only space for love.

The patients have a certain appreciation of life that comes with a cancer diagnosis. They laugh and joke together and quickly bond. They have a connection they don't share with their friends and family. They know the pain they each feel, the daily struggle they each face and they see through it; sharing stories of how far they have come, supporting those at an earlier stage in their journey and learning from those who have been walking this road for many years. It is an honour to witness and I am frequently inspired by the strength and courage of my fellow warriors.

Likewise their loved ones who visit never bring stress or drama or judgement. They bring hugs, photos, stories and laughter. They bring hope and a reminder of life outside the hospital walls. Most importantly they always, always bring love.

I am most inspired by the partners (my husband included of course). They are pillars of strength for the person they love. They comfort and soothe, bringing smiles and laughter to faces stained with tears. Their partner may no longer look the same as the day they fell in love and yet they look beyond it. In doing so they demonstrate the importance of loving a soul and not a body.

There is, of course, often sadness in their eyes. Sometimes they cry with their loved one. Sometimes they just hold them, offering a comfort that no one else on this earth could match. It's a real test of a relationship to witness. While their partner goes through treatment they have to take on every role in the family home, while also caring for an incredibly sick loved one and emotionally dealing with the implications of their diagnosis. Some of these relationships have children and they are called on to care for and reassure them also. I struggle to find the words about how beautiful and wonderful these relationships are to witness but the word 'soulmates' comes to mind. After all, once cancer strips your identity and everything you'd expected in your life together what else is left apart from two connected souls?

The same can be said of the staff. In an oncology ward there is time to get to know your patients; what makes them laugh and cry, what they are feeling, who they are as a person when you look beyond their diagnosis? Many of the patients have been on the ward more than once and, usually, for extended periods of time. As you watch the nurses laugh and joke and comfort the people in their care, it is sometimes hard to remember the pain that these caring souls also deal with too. They connect with their patients on a long and challenging journey and then are often at their side when they pass. Yet despite this they smile, offering strength and courage, hope and determination to those in the greatest of need. In minutes they can go from holding the hand of a patient hearing the news that they will soon die, to making jokes with another patient whose soul needs to be lightened with positivity. These are true angels at work and I feel so blessed to have witnessed them in action.

Love has touched so many moments of my journey while I was in hospital. It was there when the woman who cleaned my hospital room sat crying with me when I was in too much pain to get out of bed, telling me she couldn't sleep for thinking about me. It was there when an auxiliary nurse sat with me for over an hour in the middle of the night talking and showing me pictures of her grandchildren to keep me company because I couldn't sleep. It was there when a doctor talked to me about what had been happening in a shared favourite TV show while she took a heart trace which involved her seeing me naked, rather than making the situation unnecessarily awkward. I felt love from the nurse who sat with me during her breaks, even when she was working on a different ward, because she had supported me through an anxiety attack soon after my surgery and now knew me as a person. Love was there every time a person took the time to know me.

I've learnt that when at your lowest, lower than you thought humanly possible that this is all that matters; the compassion of one human to another and the care to show love to another spirit. How blessed I am to have seen this on my journey. We truly live in a wonderful world filled with hope, possibility and love. You just need to know where to look.

A Second Goodbye

For as long as I can remember, my husband has always made an excuse to say goodbye to me at least twice before he leaves the house for work. He'll embrace me, telling me to have a good day and to drive safe and then he'll make his way for the door. Then, without fail, every day, he will come across the room again saying he has to do something – hug the cat goodbye, pick up something, any excuse you can think of. Then, he will embrace me again, hugging me a little tighter and making small talk as he puts off leaving.

I used to be so busy that this would drive me insane,

especially if I was the one trying to leave the house. Since my diagnosis, however, it has become my favourite part of the day. I now realise that my husband always had it right. He always prioritised our embrace over every other second of the day. He was holding on to the brief moment for just a few seconds longer. It's now my happiest part of the day and if he were ever to leave without a second goodbye, it would break my heart.

Although he may not realise it, my husband had been highlighting the importance of these moments together. He had been showing me that the only moments in our day that really matter are when we are with those that we love. Above all, he was highlighting that we never know when we are exchanging our final embrace and that each and every time we leave a loved one we should treat it as a final goodbye.

These moments now mean more to me than any other. It's why I always hug my friends when I see them. It's also why I say 'I love you' not just to my husband and family but to all of the friends that I truly cherish.

In life we don't always get to experience a second goodbye so make each moment count and treat every encounter with the same love and compassion you would a final one.

CHAPTER 16: BEAUTY

Modern society, particularly in the West, often fails to teach us to love ourselves and to look after our incredible bodies with care, compassion and understanding. Instead the media often teaches us to compare ourselves to others, to judge our fellow human and to loathe the person we see in the mirror. This can result in unnecessary suffering as we desperately seek to achieve the 'perfect' body image: we don't eat when we are hungry (in order to lose weight); we exercise when we are in pain (to get fit); we don't embrace a healthy lifestyle; we are ashamed to be our authentic selves and so on.

I have been there. I have hated my body. I have felt shame when I looked in the mirror. I have punished myself with food and exercise. Now, however, I say enough is enough! I hadn't realised how much importance I had placed on my appearance until I lost everything that served my physical form. However, there is nothing like losing a third of your body weight and all of your hair and eyebrows to make you realise that the people that really love you don't care what you look like so long as you are healthy.

I now believe that it is essential that we start to love our bodies for the wonderful, life-giving resources that they are, rather than punishing ourselves because we don't look like the flawless images we see in the media.

If you do nothing else today, do yourself a favour and bin your scales, take a good long look at yourself in the mirror and tell yourself how gorgeous you are.

The Exchange

I'd like you to take a moment to think over an important question.

How much value do you place on your life? Or, let me ask you another way, what payment would you make to live? What would you consider the appropriate cost of your survival?

I'm not talking about monetary value. Death doesn't work in currency. I'm talking about something much more precious that that.

Would you pay with your dignity? Your looks perhaps? How about your strength? Would you use your career as payment? What about your hobbies? Would you offer up your sense of self or your body image? What about parts of your body? Would you offer up some of your organs or your limbs?

At what point would the payment get too much? At what point would you choose to not pay the fee and to finally offer up your life instead?

It's a question we don't ever expect to have to answer, however, it's a question most cancer warriors face at some point in their journey. Every choice about survival comes at a price, an adjustment, a sacrifice, a new way of living.

In this exchange between life and death we discover who we are. We discover what truly matters to us and, above all, we discover that the most valuable thing we possess is not our looks, our career, our house or our possessions. It is being alive. It is life itself.

You see, in reality, nothing else matters. The purpose of life is to live with joy and kindness and love in our hearts in all that we do. This knowledge is what cancer gave me in return for the payments I made. Today, I am living the best and most fulfilling days of my life not in spite of cancer, but because of it!

My payments started small. I gave my hair, my strength, and my sense of wellbeing. I exchanged my hobbies, my career and even some friendships. The payment demands constantly grew. Before long I was exchanging organs for my life. These payments came with hidden charges and I continued to pay with my pain, fatigue and weakness. Were the payments worth it?

Sometimes I thought they weren't. Sometimes I thought I couldn't take it any more. I wanted out. I wanted to stop these payments, these exchanges. At these moments I was gifted love and kindness and hope from those around me. This made the payments easier and, in the end, the people I love made the payments worth it.

The resulting gift of my own life, the gift of waking up each morning and welcoming a new day, of knowing what the true meaning of life is, of knowing what matters most to me in the whole world is worth every single second of pain; every moment of fear; every breath of despair. This is what life is and it's up to us to live it.

Be Proud of Your Body

Ovarian cancer. Surgery. Chemotherapy. Hair loss. Wheelchair. Intensive care. Terminal. Incurable. Remission. Scars. So many words and phrases have entered my world since I was diagnosed. Some have been easier to deal with than others. But one word stood out because I had never heard it before: colostomy.

I didn't even know what a colostomy was before my operation. No one in my life had ever mentioned this word before. After some questioning and research, however, I discovered 'colostomy' meant life changing surgery.

For those of you who are unfamiliar with what this is, it basically means that the surgeons had removed part of my large intestine and diverted this into an opening (known as a stoma) in my tummy. This would mean that rather than my intestine ending at my anus it would now end via my tummy to the left of my belly button. So as to prevent inevitable mess, I was told I would have to always wear a small pouch known as a colostomy bag over the stoma to collect waste products. As the stoma wouldn't have muscle control like an anus, the bag would have to be worn at all times. I was devastated.

I didn't have bowel cancer. I had ovarian cancer.

As I have already detailed, it turns out that ovarian cancer doesn't hang around in just the ovaries. It likes to spread to other organs. In my case, it had moved throughout my abdominal and chest cavities and, as a result, part of the surface of my bowel would need to be cut away.

In the days following my surgery I faced drain sites, drips, syringe drivers, an 18-inch scar and a colostomy. As the days turned to weeks these additions slowly diminished. The drains were removed. The scar started to heal and fade. The drips were wheeled away. But one thing remained: the colostomy wasn't going anywhere. It was a permanent feature.

It was hard to come to terms with. It felt like the final shred of the little dignity I had left had been removed as I no longer even had control over my bodily functions.

In a 'normal' body you are able to control when you poo by using the muscles in your anus. Your colon, however, doesn't have muscles that you can consciously control. So if you have a colostomy your body excretes waste whenever it wants. Any time. Any place. No warning. No control. Great! So I learned that I'd now need to carry spare colostomy bags with me wherever I went so that if my bag filled I could change it.

I was given a special card stating that I had a medical condition that allowed me access to any toilet, anywhere - one small perk. I was also given a special 'radar key' that allowed me to unlock any public toilet - okay another small perk.

I was taught that I could no longer wear my usual, low rise, button up jeans as they can cut off the bag and prevent it from working and would instead have to wear high waisted jeans, jeggings or dresses. I suddenly had an excuse to buy a whole new wardrobe. No questions asked. Things were starting to look up!

While it was hard to come to terms with at first, I began to realise that this was a result of life-enhancing surgery. Would I, if given the chance, turn back time and say 'no wait, actually could you just leave that cancer on my bowel as I'd rather have cancer than a colostomy?' Hell no!

A great comfort for me during this time was to look at pictures of other people online who had a stoma and were 'working it'. To my great surprise there were many beautiful souls strutting their stuff and displaying their stomas proudly for all to see as they posed for pictures.

With time and support, I began to realise that it wasn't such a big deal after all. I mean, let's be honest, would I rather leave cancer in my body and not have a stoma? Of course not! Since my operation I have completely adjusted to life with my 'tum hole', as my hubby affectionately calls it, and now actively campaign to show that stomas are no big deal and, more importantly, you can still be sexy with a stoma. If nothing else they are a great excuse to buy a whole new wardrobe.

Of course there are still hard times. Like when I go to use a disabled toilet and I'm judged by observers because I don't 'look' disabled. Having an upset tummy is the worst! Usually when you have an upset tummy you will get enough time (hopefully) to find a toilet. Not with a colostomy. There is no warning. Waste will make an exit whether you like it or not! If your bag sticks in place, great. If not then all hell is breaking loose wherever you are! I've had to bin a few outfits as a result of what one of my nurses affectionately refers to as a 'code 20'. I've learned that having a dark sense of humour helps.

What also helps is people sharing their story about their colostomies. Did you know one in 500 people in the UK have a colostomy? And not just because of cancer. Sometimes because of Crohn's disease or even from childbirth. With this in mind I'm pretty sure you know someone with a colostomy bag. But there is still so much stigma attached to discussing 'poo'.

So what can we do?

We can celebrate the differences in our bodies. We can stop being embarrassed by our bodies and what they do. We can stop body shaming. And, most importantly, we can stop taking everything so seriously.

I am no longer ashamed of my body or indeed of my colostomy. Instead, I am proud of it. How lucky I am that I have access to life-saving surgery and medical advancements that have enabled my surgeons to do the fantastic job they've done.

I was asked recently if I would have a colostomy reversal operation if I were to be offered. 'No,' came my instinctive response. You see I've grown to love my colostomy. It saved my life and it is a reminder every day how lucky I am to be alive. Also, as disgusting as many people may think it is, at the end of the day everybody poos. It's just some of us are lucky enough to be able to do it 'on the go'!

See, I told you a sense of humour helps.

Be A Role Model

I haven't grown to love my scars. In fact, I loved them from the very first day I had them. I wasn't ashamed of them. Instead I knew that they had given me life. They tell an incredible story of survival. Similarly I embraced my bald head while going through chemotherapy. I saw a warrior when I looked in the mirror. I never saw a victim.

Yet if I were to believe what society and the media have told me then I would be feeling very differently. I would view my scars as ugly and hide them from the world. My colostomy bag would be disgusting and I would feel ashamed. When I was bald I would have felt less of a woman.

Eh, hold on a minute. I don't think so!

I have never felt more wonderful than I do today. I've never felt more proud of my body for all of the incredible things it can do and that, most importantly, it is providing me with life. My body is incredible, and so is yours!

So, why does society often tell us otherwise? Why do so many of us feel we need to be a certain weight, not to be healthy but to be attractive? Why are we often made to feel less than ourselves unless we look a certain way? Where are all the role models telling us that our gorgeous 'imperfections' make us perfect?

When I was a little girl growing up every female role model looked a certain way. She had her pretty dress and her long perfect hair. She was beautiful and slim. The dolls I played with, the cartoon characters I admired, they were all the same. Nothing changed when I became a teenager, or even when I became an adult. Everywhere I looked I was told that 'beauty' and 'perfection' looks a certain way.

Now I am wondering where are the cartoon characters with a little (or a lot) of curves on their hips? Where are the dolls rocking a short hairstyle, or no hair at all for that matter? Where are the models with scars? Where are the actors or actresses with colostomy bags? Ultimately, where are the people teaching the next generation that being a warrior, being 'different' and 'imperfect' is much more sexy than being 'perfect'.

On my journey I always aspire to be the person I needed when I was growing up. I want to challenge society's perception of 'perfect' and encourage us all to embrace our beautiful bodies.

It took cancer, chemotherapy and massive surgery before I appreciated my body and learned to love it without bashing it every time I looked in the mirror. Wouldn't it be wonderful if the next generation just unashamedly loved themselves for who they are?

I want to see role models that real people can relate to. There needs to be a change and it starts with you the next time you look in the mirror and recognise how incredibly gorgeous, sexy and wonderful you are.

You don't need to look a certain way or weigh a certain weight. You don't have to fit into a certain dress size or wear 'the latest fashion'. You, just as you are, right now, are already perfect.

Let Yourself Shine

I chose to mark the Winter Solstice of 2017 by gathering around a fire pit in our garden with a group of incredible women. In turn we each wrote on scraps of paper (pink of course) what we wished to leave behind as we moved into the new season. In some sort of informal ceremony we shared stories with one another about what we were letting go of as we let the pieces of paper fall victim to the flames.

While I shared this experience with these inspiring women, I was struck by the similarity of what we were each letting go of, despite our different paths.

As we each took it in turns to describe the adversities in our lives - work, relationships, grief, illness and more - words like 'guilt', 'shame', 'anxiety', 'worry' and 'fear' dropped repeatedly into the flames and I couldn't help but wonder why so many of us (myself included) carry these burdens around with us; this overwhelming preoccupation of worrying about what others think, of wanting to please everyone all of the time at the expense of our own joy and, most importantly, letting society dim the light in our hearts so as to not offend or upset those around us.

The trouble with dimming our light, however, is we stop letting our heart sing, we stop feeling joy and, in doing so, we slowly start to die. At first this is only metaphorical, of course, however the more we switch off to and deny our true self for the sake of 'fitting in', the more dis-ease we let into our bodies and into our lives. It is, without doubt, my belief that denying my true self the opportunity to shine is one of the reasons I developed cancer so young.

The trouble is that so many of us do this. So many of us try to fit in with what society thinks is 'best' and 'right' and 'expected'. But what if we all started to follow our hearts? What if one-by-one we let our hopes, and our fears, out into the world for all to see? What if we broke down the walls we had so carefully built around our hearts and let our true selves shine?

Society would change and we would no longer be expected to dull our light. We would be expected to SHINE!

Help others to shine brighter by allowing yourself to shine and, maybe, together we can make the world sparkle.

CHAPTER 17: KINDNESS

In the weeks that followed my surgery my seven year old nephew organized a charity coffee morning with the help of his mum (my sister) and some of her friends. The plan was simple; half of the money raised would go to ovarian cancer research and the other half would go to my hubby and me so that we could treat ourselves during my recovery.

While this was the loveliest offer ever, I had other plans. I couldn't bring myself to use the money on myself. Just because I had cancer didn't mean that I was any more deserving than anyone else. So, instead, I found myself thinking about what we could do with the money so that it would benefit others.

As I mulled it over, I was reading an inspiring book gifted to me by a friend entitled 'The Power of Kindness' by Piero Ferrucci, and it gave me an idea. What if I used the money to do random acts of kindness for complete strangers? Not only would this fill me with happiness because I would get to surprise people and see them smile but it would also remind people that there is good in the world and that there is always something to be grateful for. This became the start of what would become my 'random act of kindness journey'.

I bought some teal envelopes and had some business cards made with the symptoms of ovarian cancer printed on them. I figured why not also spread awareness of this type of cancer whilst also spreading love and kindness. Then, into each envelope I placed £10 or £20 and one of the cards.

The next step was to start handing them out. I remember so clearly my first random act of kindness (RAOK) delivery. I was sitting having lunch with my hubby. It was the first time we had properly ventured out of the house following my surgery and I was people-watching and taking in everything that daily life has to offer. I started to notice that everyone around us was busy on their phones and not really enjoying the moment. That is, all except two ladies who were sitting at a table near us. These ladies were laughing and joking and their positive energy filled the room. I knew then that I wanted to give them my first envelope. So, on our way out I approached their table and placed it between them. I was so nervous but as soon as I was out on the street I squealed with delight. It had been such a happy rush. The best £20 I'd ever spent!

I didn't expect anything to come of it but the two ladies posted their experience on social media and overnight it was shared more than 500 times. The story was picked up by the local press and before long I found myself chatting to these wonderful souls. It didn't end there. As a completely unexpected thank you these amazing women then did a bungee jump for Macmillan Cancer Support, raising over £4000. Inspiring to say the least!

Since then the ripples of kindness have continued to grow. I have now handed out over forty envelopes and each time I am amazed at all of the wonderful things that have since happen as a result. In fact I could have written a book dedicated just to this (and maybe one day I will). I have made new friends, spoken at events, shared emotional stories with complete strangers, been on TV and radio shows talking about my journey and had many more people raise money for charities in my name.

Most incredibly of all, many of the people who have received my envelopes, and those who have read the stories, have started to hand out their own RAOKs. As a result there are now little kindness fairies spreading love and kindness (and the symptoms of ovarian cancer) across the world! One man even signs his envelopes 'Love, Grandad' after I wrote in a blog post about our encounter that I had given him an envelope because he reminded me of my much loved, late Grandfather. Everyone always reports back how wonderful handing out a RAOK envelope makes them feel, agreeing with me that joy is found in giving and connecting with others, rather than in receiving.

Incredibly, people have also made donations to my RAOK pot and so the original fund continues to grow and my pile of envelopes never seems to shrink, despite me constantly handing them out.

People sometimes ask me why I do this and the answer is simple. I refuse to let my life become depressing just because I have a late stage cancer diagnosis. Instead I choose to spend my time making other people happy. In times of great global uncertainty isn't the most important thing we can do for society to be kind to one another other?

Handing out these envelopes has been one of my greatest joys and, without doubt, it has helped me to stay positive throughout my journey. More often than not the recipients contact me to share their story of how the act has touched their lives. In these moments I am gifted a glimpse into their world. It is always an honour and a privilege and each encounter still touches my heart.

Above all, with each encounter, I am taught more and more about the love of people and their desperate desire to be kind to one another. I struggle to put into words the profound effect that these acts of kindness have had on me. I can remember each encounter and each person's story. I feel a deep connection with each of them for the role they have played in lifting my spirits on what could have been an otherwise awful journey.

I think the easiest way for you to understand how incredible it is to connect with strangers in this way is simply by handing out your own RAOKs. You never know how much of an impact you will have on the recipient. To give you an example I have copied one of the many messages I have received. May it touch your heart in the same way it touched mine and offer you a reminder that kindness still exists in the world, it's up to us to spread it.

'I wanted to thank you for a random act of kindness you probably haven't even realised you have given me; one that means more and has changed my life more than any other amount of notes in an envelope.

Meeting you sparked something in me, inspiring me to see the wonderful, the joy and the good in the world. I've never been an overly negative person; in fact until I met you I would have said I was positively positive but I was positively positive about the big things. I had become so busy and hectic that I was missing the wonderful that happens every day and when times got tough, although I never became down, I let my spirits become dampened and saw things as a tough challenge I had to work through that I wouldn't enjoy but I would do because it would need doing.

Before meeting you my life was really good, I was positive, happy, had everything I wanted, but I lacked contentment, I always wanted more whether from my career or my life and I would give myself a hard time to achieve these things. Throughout all this I lost sight of the everyday amazing; a sunrise, a walk in the park, watching the birds, singing my favourite song full blast in the car at traffic lights and not giving a single fuck!

I worried constantly about things I couldn't control, about others' choices and behaviours, but that day you gave me that envelope started something for me, I started to read your blogs and I started to think differently. I started to think if you can let go of what you can't control and you can find happiness in the everyday amazing in the face of such challenge then I really have no excuse. And so I did.

This was conscious at first, an effort every day to acknowledge something wonderful, something amazing, to do something for someone without expecting anything in return; that feeling you gave me when I handed out that first envelope just ran through me and I was hooked. So I did and I have and I will.

Every morning now starts the same, I drive to work, radio full blast, screeching my heart out at the top of my lungs to my favourite songs. I don't care that I am sat at the traffic lights for all to see, often it raises a smile, perhaps starting someone else's day on a positive. Each morning I give a nod to the sun as it rises over the mountains as I wind down through the roads, and each day I smile and acknowledge how wonderful it is to be here another day.

After that, the day can go a number of ways, but then it always ends the same way, with a huge feeling of contentment and happiness but mostly just grateful for another pretty amazing day with the people I love.

Meeting you has taught me this and it is a lesson I am glad I have learnt as in all truth nine months ago I would have told you I was as happy as I could be. I was positive and had everything I ever wanted, but now I see it was the one thing that money, careers or those round about me could not give me or buy me that I was missing, seeing the wonderful in every day. These are the things that have brought me true happiness. I can honestly say this is the happiest I have ever been, when on face value this had the potential not to have been a great year.

I now truly dance like no one is watching, sing like no one is listening and love and care without worry of what others will think. It's been so liberating and has truly set me free bringing with it all the things I strived for in my career and life without giving myself a hard time to get them. It is almost like my soul is rewarding me for giving it a break! Thank you.'

LIVE LIKE YOU WERE DYING

From the very start my cancer was labelled as 'terminal or 'incurable' and I was often referred to as 'dying' in the media and yet, to me, I was more alive than I'd ever been before. Where was this disconnection coming from? Why had the word cancer taken away the possibility that I could still be living until the moment I actually took my final breath?

I recall bumping into an old friend a few months after my diagnosis.

'I heard the news and thought you'd just be bed bound now,' they explained, looking shocked at the fact I was not only out of my house but, in fact, on a walk with my dog over a mile from home.

'I'm not dead yet,' I responded with a laugh.

This belief has been my 'go to' ever since. As long as I am breathing, I am living and I plan to do so to the

287

fullest of my capabilities for as long as I can.

Since my diagnosis I have witnessed countless people touched by death. Either they have been told they have cancer for the first time, or their cancer has returned. Some have early stage cancer and others, like me, have late stage cancer. In each encounter it never ceases to amaze me how death illuminates a person's spirit. You see, you cannot hide or fake your true personality once death walks beside you. You are stripped bare of your defenses and are exposed to life.

Through observation of these encounters, I have become very aware of the 'living dead'. No I'm not talking about zombies, (much to my husband's dismay as I'm sure he'd much rather they were the topic of this book) I'm talking about those people who die before they are dead. People who live in fear waiting for the day death will take them. For me, death already has them, for even though they are still breathing they have clearly ceased to live.

Everyone responds differently of course. Others love the challenge of having death walking beside them. Its presence offers them a reminder to live and instead of being scared, they are more alive than ever before. This, for me, is the true meaning of living. It is to live in the face of death. It is to live your life as if you were dying.

In reality, of course, death walks beside us all. Whatever your current health situation, you and I have one startling reality in common: we both have an expiry date and we are both going to die. We are, in fact, just like everyone else. We are terminal. Having stage four cancer does not guarantee that my expiration will be reached before someone else without cancer. Instead, it provided me with a wake up call that life is for living. It is not a dress rehearsal. And, for that, I am truly grateful for my cancer diagnosis for waking me up to the fact that I had spent the previous 30 years dead!

Death has now become a welcome presence in my life. It acts as a daily reminder for me to truly live. You see the knowledge that death is walking beside me has made me undeniably aware of my own mortality and the fact that one day I will die. It has made me realise that if I want to fulfill my dreams then it is now or never. This is it.

It is for this reason that I chose to conclude this book by sharing the lessons that facing death has brought me, in the hope that they will help you to choose to live.

Death may walk beside me now on every step of my journey but, don't get me wrong, I'm not wallowing in a constant fear, depressed and unable to live. No, that would mean that the beautiful lessons cancer has brought me have been ignored. Instead I am aware of its whispers. I hear it call my name in the quiet moments of pain, in the dead of night, punctuating my daily joy with subtle reminders of its permanent presence.

Internally I scream, 'I heard you. I learned the lessons. Now hear me. I want to LIVE!'

It can be such a cruel reality; the gift of knowing how precious life is, the wanting to live and enjoy every moment coinciding with the fact that your life will be shortened by this gift. Oh the painful irony.

Perhaps, however, that is part of the beauty of stage four Cancer. Perhaps if remission meant 'never to return' instead of 'short break' then the lessons wouldn't be learned. Time would march on and slowly we'd slip into old habits, forgetting the value of each moment, of each breath.

In the incredible book 'When Breath Becomes Air' the author perfectly explains 'there is cancer and then there is CANCER', highlighting the difference between those who have curable cancer and go on to live happy, healthy lives and those who, like so many of us, have incurable cancer which will linger in the shadows ready to pounce.

No one else wants to talk about it. Your loved ones can fear bringing up the topic of death and in doing so can further feed your fears. I wanted to discuss my death with the people I love, not because I was sad or worried but because I wanted to be heard. I wanted them to know, and understand, the reality. I wasn't scared of my death. I was scared that they hadn't accepted that my death was a possibility. I felt a self-inflicted responsibility to protect them weighing me down. I wanted to normalise the situation so that we could be prepared in whatever way was right for us. Instead, however, I kept my thoughts inside. I chose to protect them while frantically screaming inside with a desperate need to be heard.

Then, when I least expected it, a friend said 'we'll look after Ewan when you're gone.' The acceptance, the acknowledgment of the reality of my diagnosis was the most comforting words I'd ever heard. They didn't depressingly insinuate that my death was imminent, neither did they ignorantly suggest I would live forever. No, what they did was reassure me. With those words they also silently said, 'I hear your fears, I love you, I support you, I'm here'.

I was not as alone as I'd once thought. They knew. They accepted. And suddenly I realised: perhaps everyone 'knows'.

Had I really thought talking about it would make any difference? Is that what I wanted? To dwell on my death instead of enjoying my life.

Perhaps all of us in this journey together - we cancer warriors and those who love us - can do is savour each moment, each smile, each breath without anticipatory grief of an unknown future.

Yes, perhaps that's all any of us can do. Each and every one of us on this wild and wonderful journey called life. We can live for today, irrespective of tomorrow, and pause and smile at all of the wonderful, incredible and beautiful moments there are to feel grateful for.

You see living in fear of your death doesn't change anything. However, living like you are dying can change your whole world and allow you to welcome and accept all that is beautiful in your life and to finally give yourself permission to follow your dreams.

As I write these words, the main thing is that I feel

well, I feel healthy and, above all, I am still doing the things that I love.

In the words of Jon Kabat-Zinn -

'As long as you are breathing, there is more right with you than wrong with you, no matter how ill or how hopeless you may feel.'

My positivity won't be wavered, my hope won't be diminished and above all my joy still overflows!

As a parting thought I will leave you with this. What if cancer has a stage five after stage four? What if stage five is about finding out who you truly are? What if stage five is about LIVING?

I have embraced stage five with all of my heart. I treat my life as an adventure and I aim to spread love, kindness and positivity for as long as my heart keeps beating. I encourage you to do the same and, above all, I encourage you to live as if you were dying.

May your life be filled with love and light always and may you have the courage to pursue you dreams.

With all my love, Fi xx

HOW LONG HAVE I GOT? - AN EXCERCISE

So often we can read a book, or watch a video, that inspires us and leaves us wanting to make a change and yet we are left with the lingering question of *'how?'*

I didn't want to end my book by simply telling you to start living like you are dying. I understand this is a more than ominous thought for most. So, instead, I wanted to leave you with a quick exercise to start you on the most wonderful path you can go on - the path to truly living and awakening your soul's purpose.

I'd like you to set aside 20 minutes where you will be undisturbed to complete the following exercise. Yes, I understand your time is precious and you may have to get up 20 minutes earlier than the rest of your household but please give yourself this gift.

Now, use this precious time to answer the following questions. Remember, no one else has to see these answers. You can write them here or on a separate piece of paper. What is essential is that you are 100% honest with yourself and that you don't hold back. Dream big! I am with you, supporting your journey.

1. What would you do differently if you knew you were going to die in eighteen months time?

2. What would you change in your life if you knew you were going to die in six months?

3. What would you change today if you thought you might die tomorrow?

Now, while keeping the bigger dreams in your mind, I want you to start with your answers to question 3. Start by making the changes today that will provide you with a better tomorrow. This is how you begin to live like you are dying and, more importantly, it's how you begin to live the life your heart and soul have longed for.

So many people have asked me what difference I would like to see in the world from people reading my book. This is it. It is you making a decision to live - I mean truly live - and start enjoying your life. This is how you will best honour my words and my journey.

Because the answer to 'How long have I got?' is simple. The answer is 'today'.

So, whatever your health or situation right now, make the day good.

Trust me, it's going to be amazing!

Fi Munro, Ph.D.

USEFUL RESOURCES

Books

This list is not exhaustive. Instead, it is just a short list to get you started on your own journey with cancer.

1. 'The Cancer Whisperer' by Sophie Sabbage
2. 'When Breath Becomes Air' by Paul Kalanithi
3. 'Mum's Not Having Chemo' by Laura Bond
4. 'Radical Remissions' by Kelly A. Turner, Ph.D.
5. 'This is Going to Hurt' by Adam Kay
6. 'Anti Cancer' by David Servan-Schreiber
7. 'You Can Heal Your Life' by Louise Hay
8. 'Mind Over Medicine' by Lissa Rankin, MD.
9. 'N of 1' by Glenn Sabin
10. 'Anatomy of an Illness' by Norman Cousins
11. 'Say No To Cancer' by Patrick Holford
12. 'The Power of Kindness' by Piero Ferrucci
13. 'The Alchemist' by Paulo Coelho
14. 'The Life Changing Magic of Not Giving a F*ck' by Sarah Knight
15. 'Love, Medicine and Miracles' by Bernie Siegel

Links

https://www.targetovariancancer.org.uk

https://eveappeal.org.uk/

https://www.ovacome.org.uk/

https://ovarian.org.uk/

http://www.drkatejames.com

http://yestolife.org.uk

https://www.macmillan.org.uk

Ovarian Cancer Symptoms #THINKTEAL

The four most common symptoms of ovarian cancer are listed below, however there are additional ones such as shoulder pain and migraines to also consider.

Please contact your GP if you have any of these symptoms persistently for two weeks or more. Please ask for a pelvic examination and do not rest until you have answers.

T - toilet habit changes
E - energy levels dropping
A - abdominal pain and/or swelling
L - loss of appetite and/or weight

ACKNOWLEDGMENTS

This book would not have been possible without the help and support of some incredible people who kept me going through my journey and to whom, without doubt, I owe my life to.

To my wonderful husband, Ewan, for embracing so many changes in our life on our shared journey back to wholeness and for listening to and discussing endless research with me. Thank you for everything you do. In particular thank you for supporting me in sharing the most intimate parts of our life with others.

To my family and friends for their unwavering support and patience in all of my endeavors. I love you all more than words could ever say.

To my medical team, in particular my oncologist, for valuing me as a person throughout every step of my journey. I feel blessed every single day to have received the care and support that you offer.

To Catherine-Rose Stocks-Rankin for your friendship, love and phone calls and for helping me to come up with the title of this book.

To Claire Birbeck, Colleen Souness and Katie Hull for so lovingly proofreading my book and not laughing, too much, at some of my most ridiculous typing errors.

To Carol Bareham, my Irish teal sister and warrior, thank you so much for your guidance, humour and support. We are in this shit together!

To all those who supported my holistic journey back to wholeness, through various treatments and therapies. Thank you all for helping me to heal.

To everyone who reads my blog and follows me on social media. Your support has given me strength through what, without you, could have become a dark time beyond recovery. This book was only possible because of you.

To my wonderful, beautiful, funny niece and nephews to whom I owe my life for their continued love, joy and hope. Jack, Sam, Lily and Ben you give me a reason to live. Thank you.

To all of my fellow cancer warriors and those who love them. May your light always shine brightly for all to see.

Finally, to all of you who supported my fundraising campaign that enabled me to receive Avastin privately. You literally helped to save my life.

ABOUT THE AUTHOR

Fi Munro, Ph.D. is a multi-award winning researcher, author, mentor and public speaker recognised internationally for her presentations and articles on her journey and the importance of maintaining holistic health.

In January 2016 she was diagnosed with stage four ovarian cancer. Since then she has been featured in two TV documentaries, in countless TV and radio shows, in newspaper and magazine articles and has been interviewed by reporters from across the globe with the intent of sharing her story with others facing adversity.

Fuelled by positivity, she is passionate about the importance of maintaining a balance of physical, emotional and spiritual health.

She lives in Perthshire, Scotland with her husband, dog and two cats.

Fi Munro, Ph.D.

Connect with Fi on Facebook, YouTube, Twitter and Instagram.

@fkmunro

www.fkmunro.com

#HowLongDoIHave

Printed in Great Britain
by Amazon